Collins

Revised Edition

EXCURSIONS

Geography

8

Author
Sukanya Chakraborty

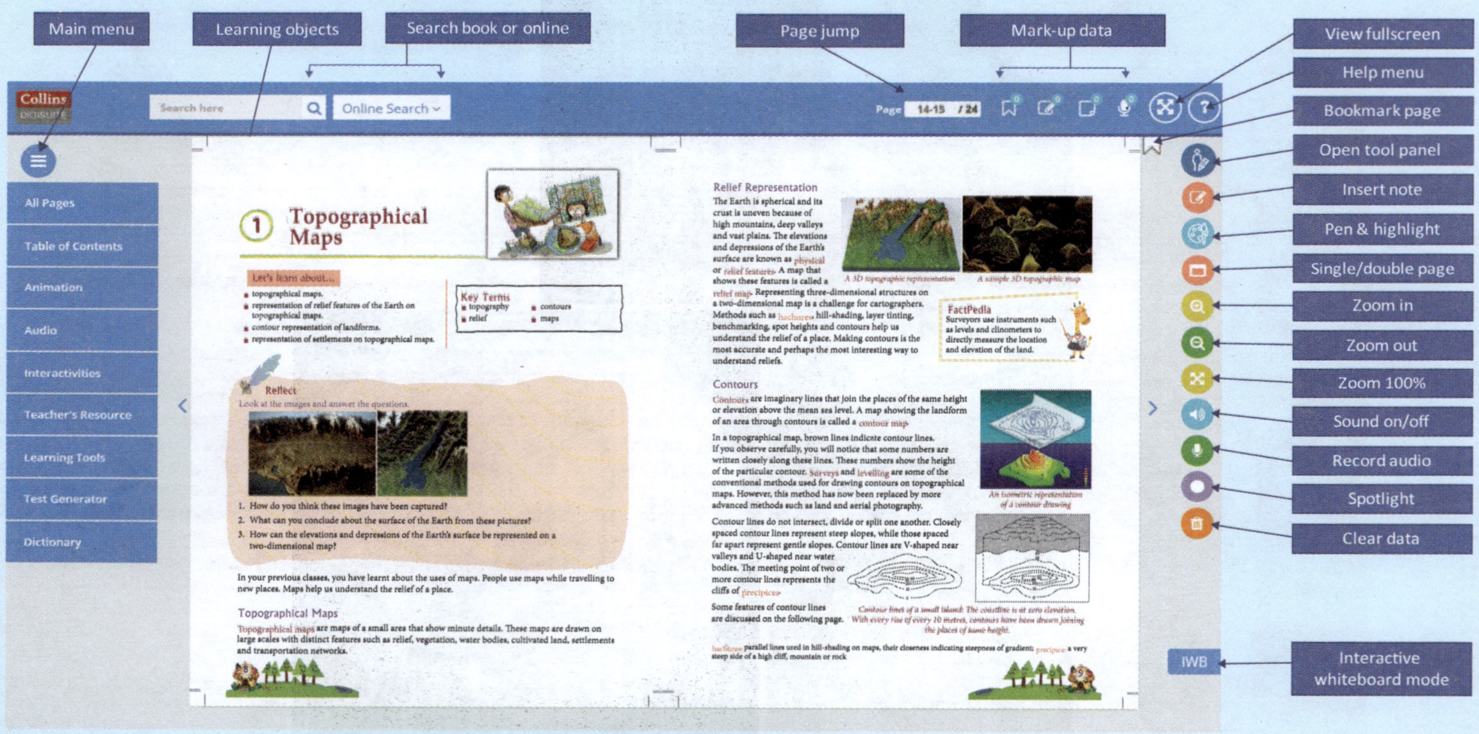

Student + Teacher			Teacher-only	
a animations	**ia** activities	**g** games	**lp** lesson plans	**tn** teacher's notes
ilt instructor-led tutorials	**w** worksheets	**v** videos	**w** worksheets	**ak** answer keys
	audio			

Preface

'Education is not the learning of facts, but the training of the mind to think.'

Albert Einstein

Excursions Revised Edition is a comprehensive course in Environmental Studies and Social Studies for young learners. This series for classes 1 to 8 has been aligned with the guidelines given in the National Education Policy, 2020. Following the curriculum, *Excursions* Revised Edition offers a course in Environmental Studies for classes 1 and 2, integrated Social Studies course for classes 3, 4 and 5 and separate Geography and History and Civics courses for classes 6, 7 and 8. The series offers features that focus on essential skills to assist learners achieve holistic learning through a multidisciplinary approach.

Each book in the series is divided into a number of themes that help students connect directly to the environment. Each theme follows a branch of geography. Practical geography deals with representation of geographical features through cartography. Physical geography focuses on understanding the Earth, its flora and fauna and atmosphere. Human and economic geography deals with the patterns and processes that shape the human society. Lastly, Regional geography addresses the unique geographical characteristics of a particular place.

This series carefully combines aspects of physical and social science as geography involves the study of the physical, biological and sociocultural environment and their relationship with human life. *Excursions* Revised Edition also provides an opportunity to the students to understand multidisciplinary links and connect their knowledge of geography to other subjects. A number of teaching methods such as case studies, application-based activities and research-based project work reinforces the concepts learnt.

About the author

Sukanya Chakraborty is a self-motivated educator with more than twenty years of experience in teaching. A Fulbright TEA fellow, she has worked at Bhavan's Nandvidya Niketan and ESSAR International School. She has planned and presented a wide range of lessons to meet the needs of various abilities and age levels. An avid geographer, Sukanya actively conducts workshops around the country.

Key Features

Varied key features in the series hone learning skills.

- **Learning** – Let's learn about, Key terms, Timeline, In a Nutshell
- **Extended learning and explanation** – Reflect, FactPedia, Figure Out, Weblinks
- **Observation and application** – DIY, Green Earth, World Connect, Geo Connect, Case Study
- **Problem-solving and analytical thinking** – Think Box, Life Skills and Values, Picture Study
- **Creativity and happiness** – Enjoy, Game
- **Multidisciplinary and holistic learning** – Across the Boundary, Snap Recap
- **Assessment and practice** – Workout, Test Yourself, Outline maps

The comprehensive teacher's resource materials are aimed at facilitating teaching and assessment. Feedback and suggestions to improve the course further are welcomed.

Key Features

Excursions Revised Edition offers features that focus on essential skills to assist learners achieve holistic learning through a multidisciplinary approach. In so doing, the series is aligned with the guidelines given in the National Education Policy, 2020.

Learning

Let's learn about...

- a globe and its uses.
- a map and its uses.
- sketch and plans.

Outlines the learning outcomes of the chapter

Key Terms

- map
- globe
- Earth
- scale
- key
- symbol
- sign
- colours
- sketch
- grid
- plan

Lists the important terms used in the chapter

In a Nutshell

South America lies totally in the Western Hemisphere. A larger part of it falls in the Southern Hemisphere.

Gives a ready reckoner to reinforce learning

Extended Learning and Application

Reflect

How have each of these innovations influenced history?

Includes warm-up tasks to initiate the learners into the topic and relate to it

FactPedia

The symbols and letters used by the Survey of India are set out in a sheet called the characteristic sheet.

Provides interesting titbits of information

Figure Out

What type of drainage patterns does your town have?

Hones referencing and research skills through small tasks

Weblinks

For more information, visit
http://mocomi.com/landforms/
Last accessed on 31/July/2020

Encourages the use of technology for extended learning

Observation and Application

Green Earth

Is ivory trade still permitted today? How does it harm nature?

Sensitizes learners towards conservation of the environment

Geo Connect

Technology has continually changed in order to meet the demands of new generations of cartographers and map users. While scientists

Helps students compare the developments of one region in relation to other parts of the world

DIY

Identify three centres of the Indus Valley Civilization in the map given below.

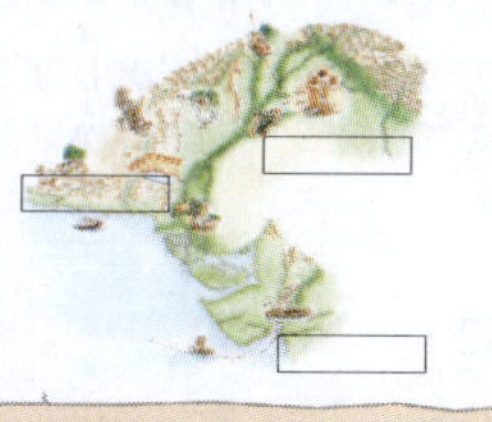

Provides application-based activities for experiential learning

Problem-solving and Analytical Tasks

Think Box

Unscramble the letters to find out the names associated with South America.

ELSSVA	....	ROOCOIN	....
XPACITOO	....	MAATCAA	....
GYRAPAUA	....	ZAONAM	....
DSEAN	....	LIBZAR	....
MAAPSP	....		

(HOTS) Facilitates out-of-the-box thinking for curious minds

Picture Study

Look at the picture and answer these questions.

1. What can you infer about the Mughal period from this painting?

Provides exercises for inferential learning

Creativity and Happiness

Enjoy

Take a print out of a world map and cut out the continents. Join their boundaries and paste them on another sheet of paper. Take a map of Pangaea and compare it to the map you created using the different continents.

Addresses wellbeing and happiness of the students through creative and fun tasks

Multidisciplinary and Holistic Learning

Across the Boundary 2

Be a Journalist

Agriculture is important as it provides food to us. We depend on farmers for this basic requirement. Do you know that the life of Indian farmers is very difficult as they work day in and day out. Imagine you are a journalist and interview a farmer based on the following issues:

- Daily work and type of crops grown in the field
- Financial management and difficulties faced
- Importance of education for farmers
- Importance of health and hygiene

Based on the information gathered, write a short report covering these points:

- The dependence of farmers on the monsoon and the difficulties ...
- Problems ...

Provides varied activities for multidisciplinary learning

Snap Recap

The Snap Recap section contains a collection of mind maps that draw the outline of the concepts that you have learned in this book. Mind mapping is a useful technique that helps you learn more effectively and improves the way that you record information. They help you see the way pieces of information fit together. Mind maps also help you remember information, as they hold it in a format that your mind finds easy to recall.

Major landforms of the Earth

- Mountains
  - Fold
- Plateaus
  - Tectonic
- Plains

Provides mind maps for quick learning

Assessment and Practice

Workout

A. Choose the correct option and fill in the blanks.

1. Egypt is situated on the banks of the river ....

To facilitate assessment

TEST YOURSELF 1

Maximum marks: 50

A. Fill in the blanks. ½×20=10

1. .... is a three-dimensional model of the Earth.
2. A detailed drawing of a small area is known as ....
3. The .... maps show a large area in a small size.
4. The science of map making is called ....
5. Rift valleys are also known as ....
6. Plains formed at the foot of the mountains are called ....
7. A shallow sea that is completely enclosed by land is called a ....
8. .... is the world's warmest ocean.
9. Plateaus are storehouse of ....
10. .... fold mountains have a lower altitude.
11. America was discovered by ....

To facilitate evaluation

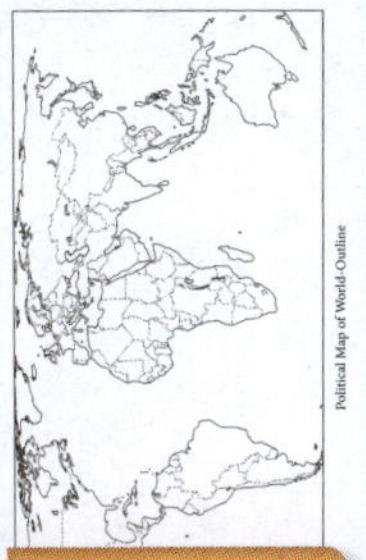

Imparts map skill practice

Contents

Theme 1

Practical Geography

Practical geography deals with the representation of geographical features through cartography. The study of the spatial distribution of relief features such as elevations, settlement and drainage patterns, vegetation and land use is the dominant aspect of this theme. To study these relief features, topographical maps of different regions published by the Survey of India are used. Therefore, the interpretation of these maps is also a part of this theme. We will interpret these maps with the help of map symbols, contour lines, contour intervals and grid references. Topographical maps give us a three-dimensional representation of the Earth's features on a two-dimensional surface.

1 Topographical Maps

Let's learn about...

- topographical maps.
- representation of relief features of the Earth on topographical maps.
- contour representation of landforms.
- representation of settlements on topographical maps.

Key Terms

- topography
- relief
- contours
- maps

Reflect

Look at the images and answer the questions.

1. How do you think these images have been captured?
2. What can you conclude about the surface of the Earth from these pictures?
3. How can the elevations and depressions of the Earth's surface be represented on a two-dimensional map?

In your previous classes, you have learnt about the uses of maps. People use maps while travelling to new places. Maps help us understand the relief of a place.

Topographical Maps

Topographical maps are maps of a small area that show minute details. These maps are drawn on large scales with distinct features such as relief, vegetation, water bodies, cultivated land, settlements and transportation networks.

Relief Representation

The Earth is spherical and its crust is uneven because of high mountains, deep valleys and vast plains. The elevations and depressions of the Earth's surface are known as physical or relief features. A map that shows these features is called a relief map. Representing three-dimensional structures on a two-dimensional map is a challenge for cartographers. Methods such as hachures, hill-shading, layer tinting, benchmarking, spot heights and contours help us understand the relief of a place. Making contours is the most accurate and perhaps the most interesting way to understand reliefs.

A 3D topographic representation

A sample 3D topographic map

FactPedia

Surveyors use instruments such as levels and clinometers to directly measure the location and elevation of the land.

Contours

Contours are imaginary lines that join the places of the same height or elevation above the mean sea level. A map showing the landform of an area through contours is called a contour map.

In a topographical map, brown lines indicate contour lines. If you observe carefully, you will notice that some numbers are written closely along these lines. These numbers show the height of the particular contour. Surveys and levelling are some of the conventional methods used for drawing contours on topographical maps. However, this method has now been replaced by more advanced methods such as land and aerial photography.

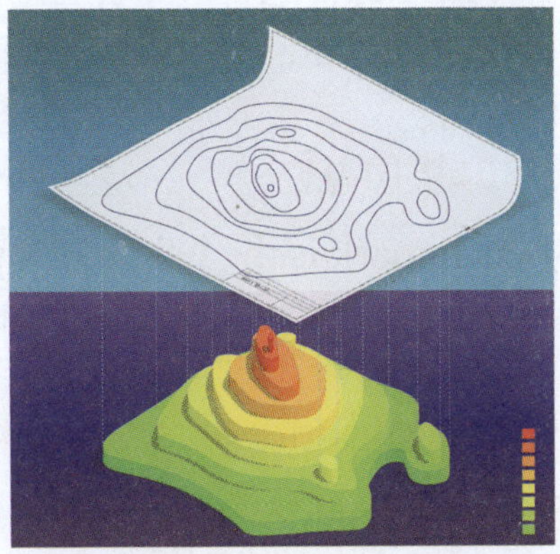

An isometric representation of a contour drawing

Contour lines do not intersect, divide or split one another. Closely spaced contour lines represent steep slopes, while those spaced far apart represent gentle slopes. Contour lines are V-shaped near valleys and U-shaped near water bodies. The meeting point of two or more contour lines represents the cliffs of precipices.

Some features of contour lines are discussed on the following page.

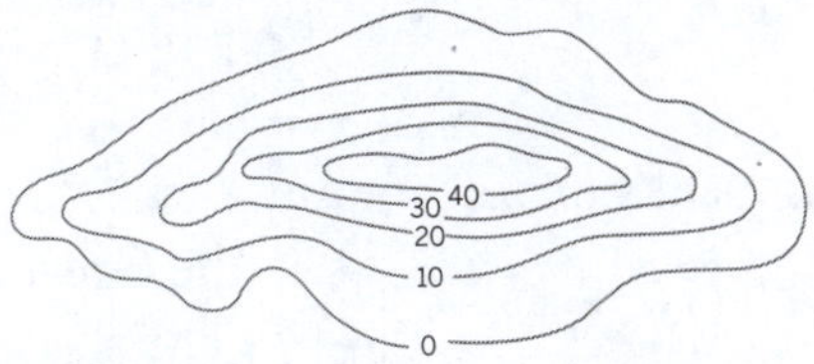

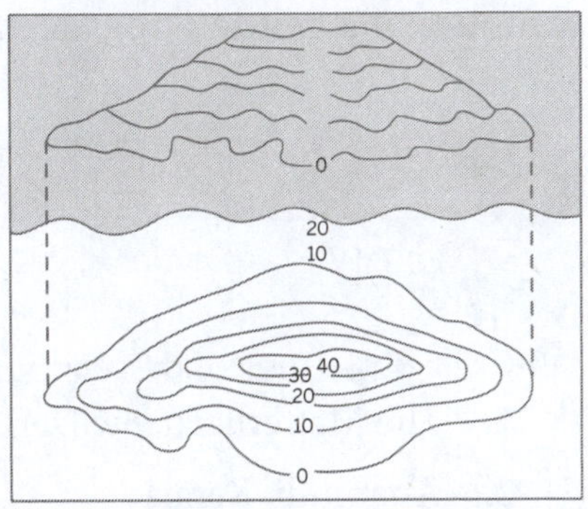

Contour lines of a small island: The coastline is at zero elevation. With every rise of every 10 metres, contours have been drawn joining the places of same height.

hachures: parallel lines used in hill-shading on maps, their closeness indicating steepness of gradient; precipice: a very steep side of a high cliff, mountain or rock

Contour interval

The distance between two consecutive contours is called contour interval (CI). The vertical distance between any two contour lines is known as vertical interval (VI). These intervals are usually constant on a given map and are measured in metres, while the vertical interval between two successive contour lines remains constant. The horizontal distance, also known as the horizontal equivalent (HE), increases when the slope is gentle and decreases with increasing height. The Survey of India uses a standard contour interval of 20 metres.

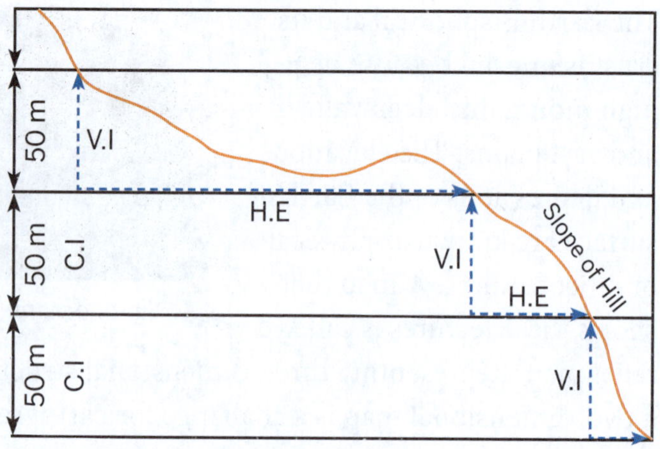

Vertical interval and horizontal equivalent

Spot height and triangulated height

Spot height is the height of random places between contours. It is represented with a dot, for example, .425. Spot heights are used to provide information about the land surface between contours and are written next to contour lines. Triangulated height is the height of a place calculated using triangle properties and trigonometry. It is represented by a small triangle, for example, Δ540.

Bench mark

Bench mark is the height of a place marked on a stone pillar or rock or shown on a building as a permanent reference. It is written using letters B and M before the number, for example, BM 200 m.

Slope of land or gradient

All topographical features show varying degrees of slopes. The steepness of a slope is called a gradient. For example, cliffs and gorges exhibit steep slopes, whereas plains exhibit gentle slopes. The slope of an area of land can be analyzed by observing the space between two consecutive contours. The contours of a gentle slope are well-spaced, and the contours of a steep slope are closely placed.

DIY

Collect pictures of these mountain peaks or volcanoes:

1. The Matterhorn, Switzerland
2. Anamudi, Kerala
3. Mauna Loa, Hawaii
4. The Great Escarpment, South Africa
5. Mount Fujiyama
6. Mount Everest

Write down the types of slopes they have.

Construction of a Topographic Profile

A topographic profile depicts relative heights, directions and types of slopes at a glance. It is used to visualize the relief of a part of land. It shows the undulation of a land surface as seen from a distance on the Earth's surface. A topographic profile is useful for making route maps for roads and railways. To construct a topographic profile, we must select a location on a map. In many cases, this location is labelled as AA' or AB.

Follow these steps to make a topographical profile:

1. Draw a section line along the contour.
2. Place the edge of a blank piece of a paper along the line and mark the starting and ending points of the line. For this profile, we have used the profile line provided, and lined it up with the profile line on the map. Any blank piece of paper can be used but it is easier to use a graph paper.

①

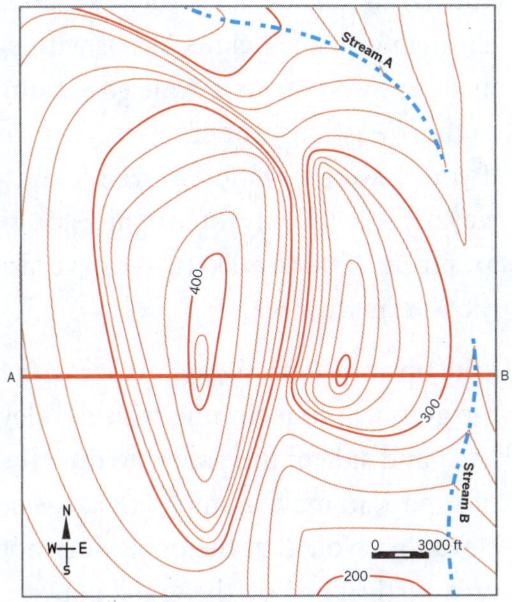

②

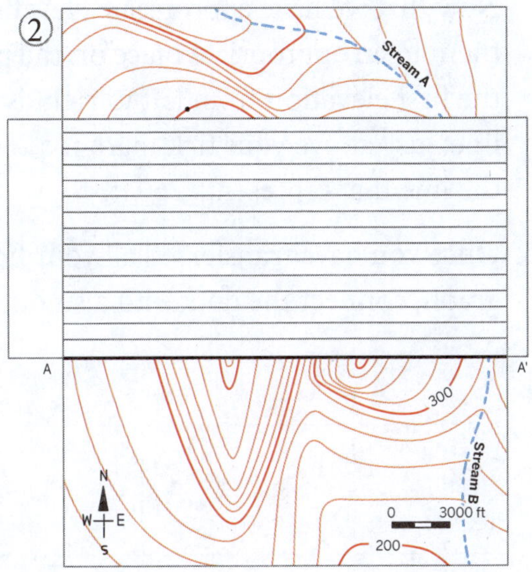

③

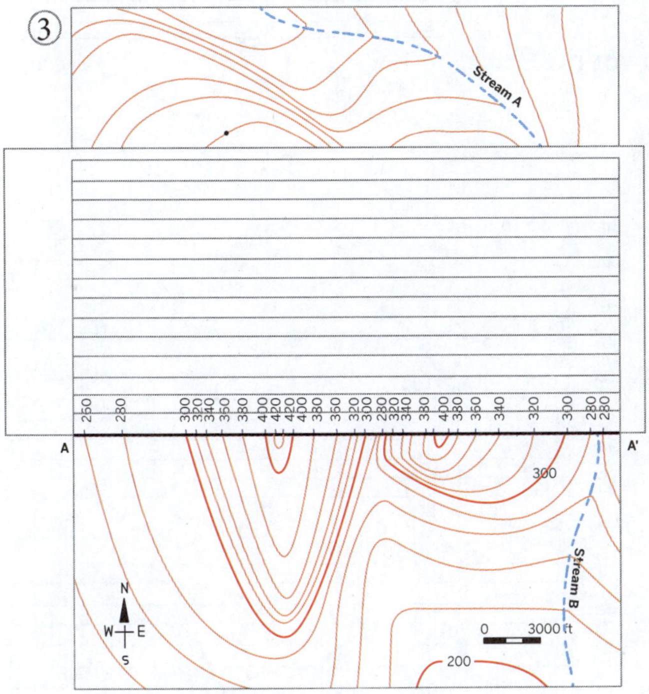

3. Start from one end and move along the edge of the paper, making a mark on the paper every time a contour line touches the edge of the paper. Make sure you label each mark with the right elevation so that you can transfer that point to the correct elevation on the graph. You may also want to mark points where rivers or streams occur.
4. Note the highest and lowest elevations recorded for later use. When you have marked all points where a contour line crosses the profile line, get a piece of graph paper. Draw a horizontal line

on the graph paper that is the length of your profile line. Draw vertical lines above your starting and ending points. Label the Y-axis with elevations making sure that your scale goes from the highest to the lowest on your cross-section. For example, if your lowest elevation is 4200 ft and your highest elevation is 7600 ft, you might want to label your axis from 4000 to 8000 ft. We have already labelled the X-axis with AA'.

④

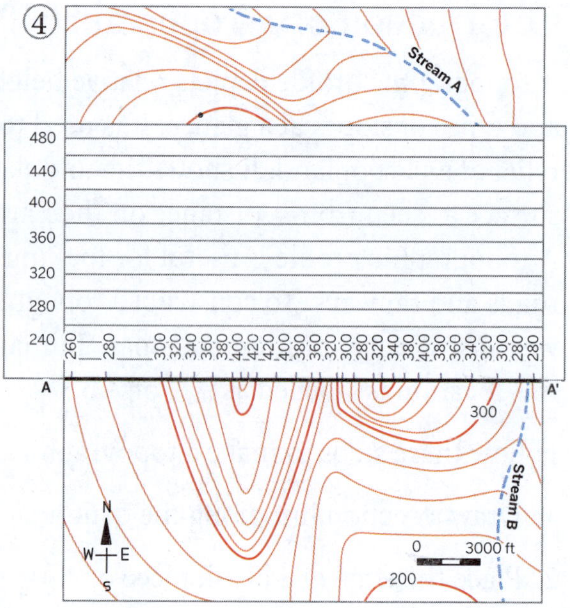

5. Line up your tick-marked paper with the bottom of the graph, and beginning with the elevation on the left-hand side of the paper, go directly up from that tick mark to make a small dot at the corresponding elevation. Note that the point does not need to be on a vertical line on the graph paper.

   Now that we have appropriate elevations, we can transfer them to an appropriate place on the plot. For example, the first elevation from left to right is 260 ft on a vertical line; just-above your tick mark for 260 ft, place a dot on the line that represents 260 ft.

⑤

6. Once you have transferred all your tick marks to your graph, connect the dots with a smooth curve.

⑥

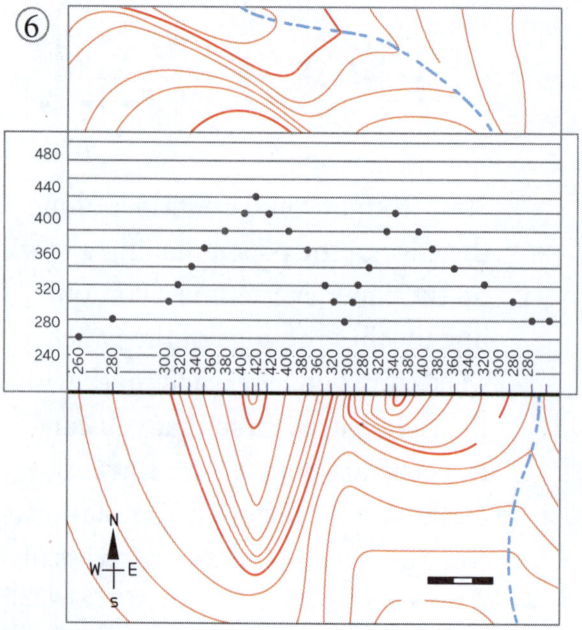

⑦

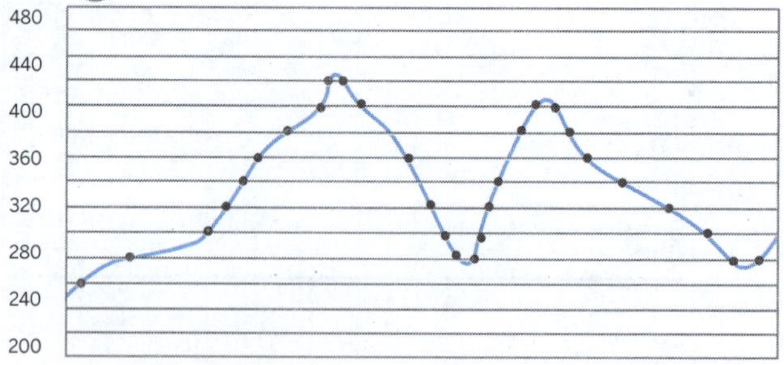

⑧

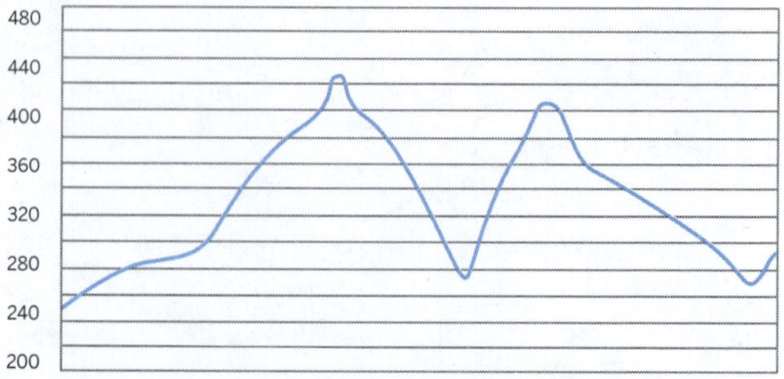

Topographical Representation of Reliefs

Mountain

A mountain is a landform where the land rises abruptly above the surrounding areas. The contours of mountains are represented with circles. The innermost circle represents the summit and the outermost circles form the broad base of the mountain.

Himalayas in Nepal

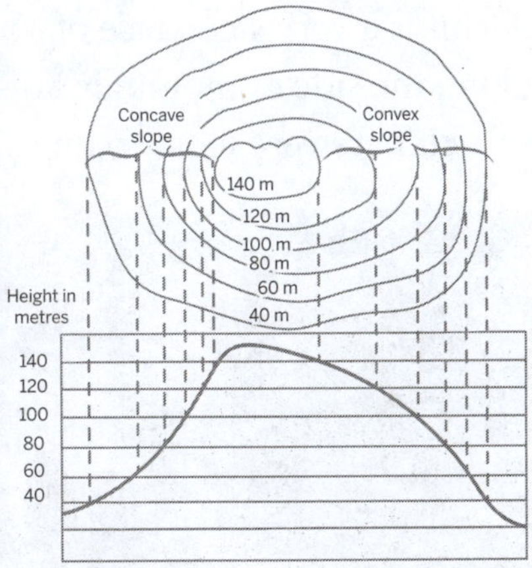

Contour lines of a mountain

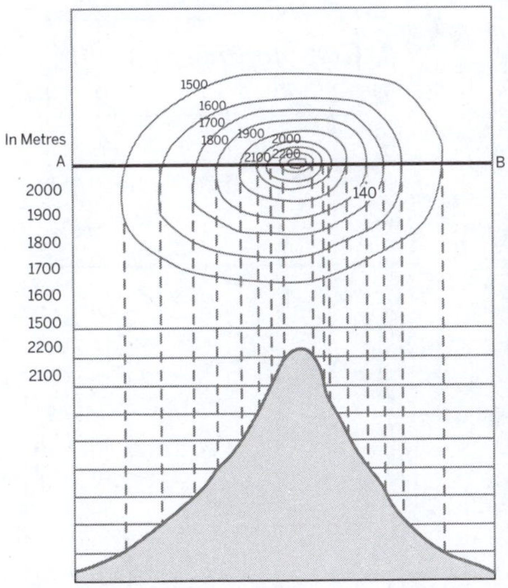

Contour lines of a conical hill

Adam's Peak, Sri Lanka

Conical hill

A conical hill is a landform that rises almost uniformly from the surrounding area. They are usually isolated but are sometimes surrounded by foothills. A conical hill with a uniform slope and narrow top is represented with concrete contours, spaced almost at regular intervals.

Plateau

A plateau is a stretched and elevated part of land with a flat top. It has a relatively steeper slope and rises above the adjoining plain or sea. Contour lines representing a plateau are elongated and elliptical. The innermost contour is broad with successive close-spaced contours.

Waterberg Plateau, Namibia

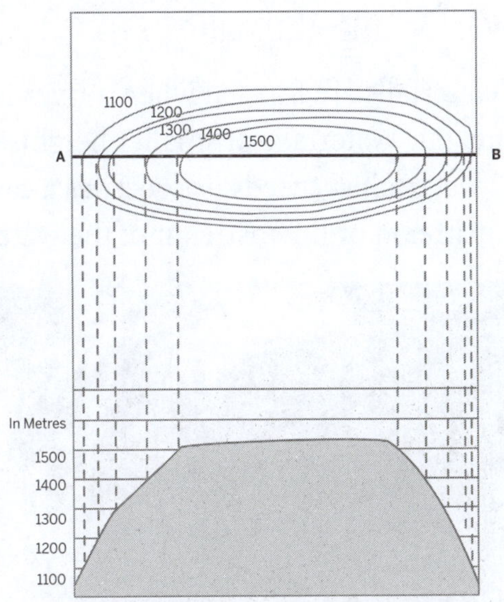

Contour lines of a plateau

Cliff

A cliff is a very steep face of rock placed at a great height, found along the side of mountains or hills. On a map, the outside contours of a cliff are very close to one another, ultimately merging into one.

Yosemite National Park, California

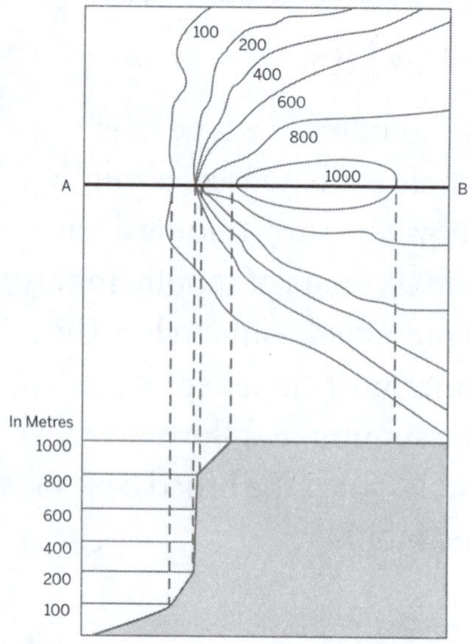

Contour lines of a cliff

Spur

Spurs are tongue-like projections that start on higher ground and end on lower ground. It is represented by V-shaped contour lines. The arms of the V point to the higher ground and the apex of the V points to the lower ground.

The Himalayas

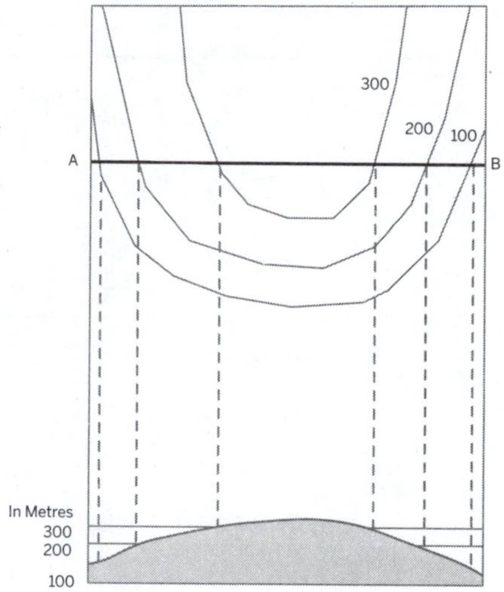

Contour lines of a spur

Waterfalls and rapids

Waterfalls are formed when a river falls abruptly from a considerable height. Waterfalls of smaller heights are called cascades. Sometimes, a waterfall succeeds or precedes a cascading stream, forming rapids upstream or downstream of the waterfall.

Baker's Falls, Sri Lanka

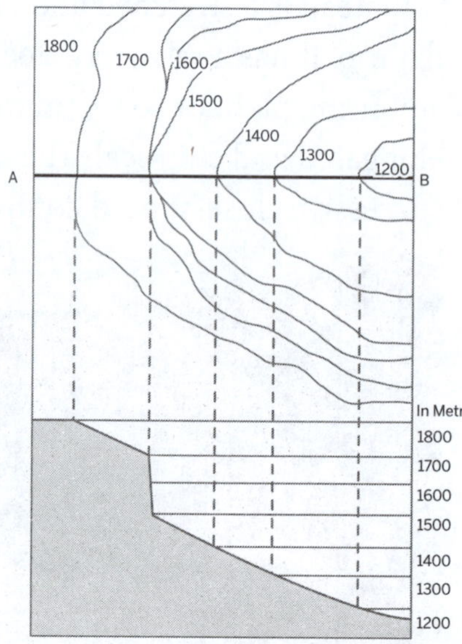

Contour lines of a waterfall

Col

If the gap between two summits of a ridge are at an altitude, it is said to be a col or a pass. It is a part of the ridge where the contours drop then rise gradually.

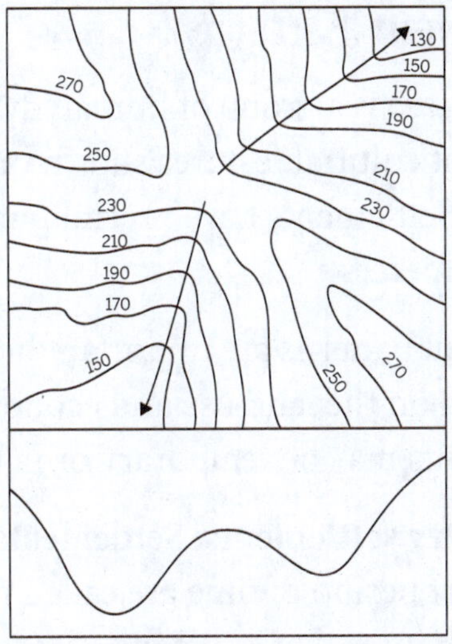

Contour lines of a col

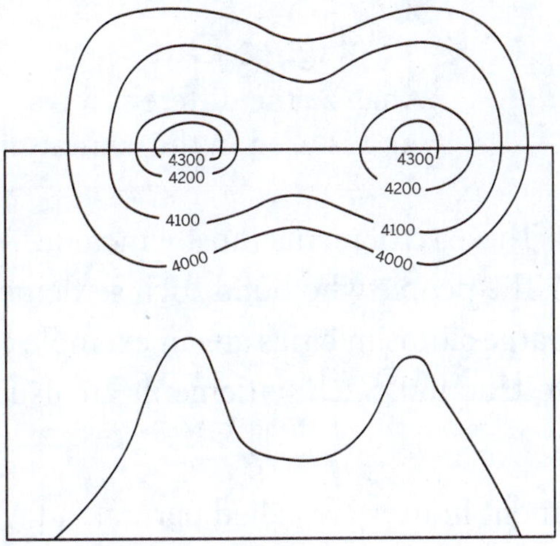

Contour lines of a saddle

Saddle

A saddle is a shallow depression between two summits with gentle slopes. It is similar to a col but contours are widely-spaced.

Ridge

A ridge is a long and narrow stretch of mountains with numerous summits. The contour lines of a ridge are placed very close to each other, forming a continuous chain of contours. The summit of each conical hill in a ridge has the same elevation.

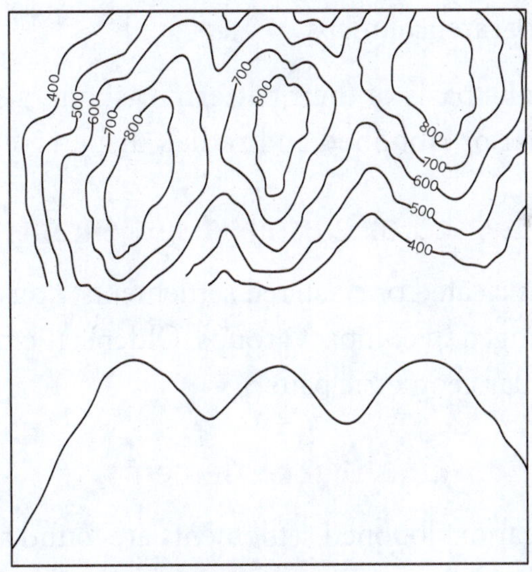

Contour lines of a ridge

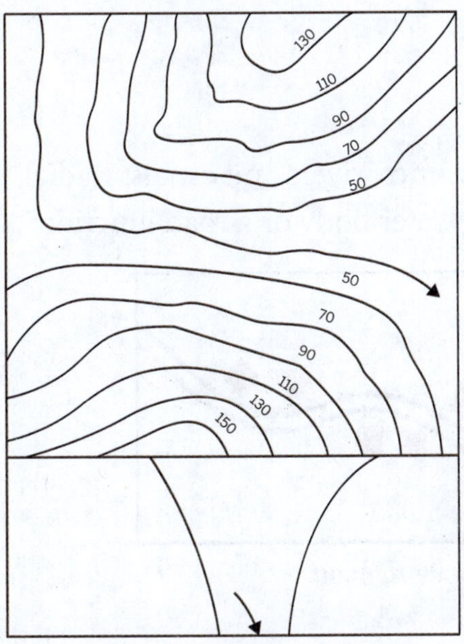

Contour lines of a gap

Gap

If the space between two summits of a ridge is very close to the valley floor, it is said to be a gap. It is similar to a col but there is a greater drop in the height, and it almost reaches the valley floor.

Settlement Patterns

A settlement is a group of human dwellings in urban and rural areas. Settlements and buildings are important cultural features shown on topographical sheets using conventional signs, symbols and colours. Settlements have several purposes—they may be residential, commercial or centres of trade and commerce.

Settlement patterns are important because they reflect a great deal on the land use and economic activities of people. Settlements may be temporary or permanent.

Figure Out

Analyze the different ways land is used in the community.

Temporary settlements: Settlements that are occupied for a short period of time are called temporary settlements. These settlements mostly include *kuchcha* houses that are made of mud, straw and tarpaulin. The people who build such settlements often migrate to other areas with better living conditions. Large slums in cities are an example of temporary settlements. They are vulnerable and prone to destruction. Such settlements are usually indicated with a square on topographical maps (□).

Permanent settlements: Places where people build permanent houses are called permanent settlements. Cities like Kolkata, Bengaluru, Mumbai, Delhi and Chennai have a large number of permanent settlements. The houses in these settlements are made of construction materials such as cement, concrete and iron. These settlements are represented with red squares (■) on topographical maps.

On the basis of their pattern or shape, settlements can be classified as nucleated or clustered; linear or ribboned and radial, dispersed or scattered.

Nucleated or clustered settlements

In nucleated or clustered settlements, houses are built very close to each other and dwellings are arranged in compact groups. Older settlements are irregular, whereas new settlements follow a regular geometric pattern.

Linear and radial settlements

Linear or ribboned settlements are found along roads, railway lines, rivers and canals. Radial settlements are spread around a central point, usually along a water body or a road junction.

Nucleated settlement

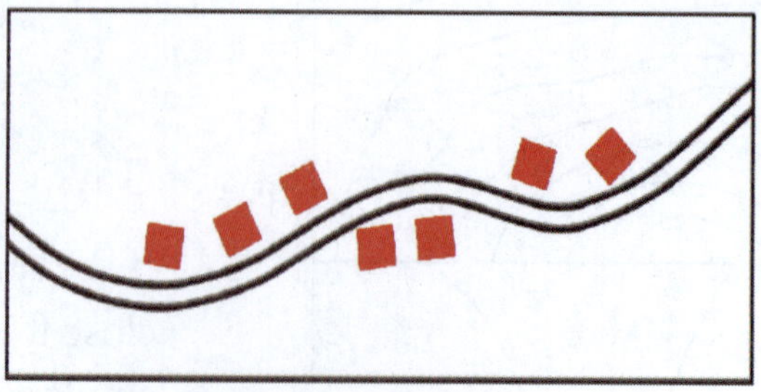

Linear settlement

tarpaulin: heavy-duty waterproof cloth, originally made of tarred canvas

Dispersed or scattered settlements

In dispersed or scattered settlements, dwellings are scattered and built at a distance. These settlements are usually found in valleys and the foothills of mountains.

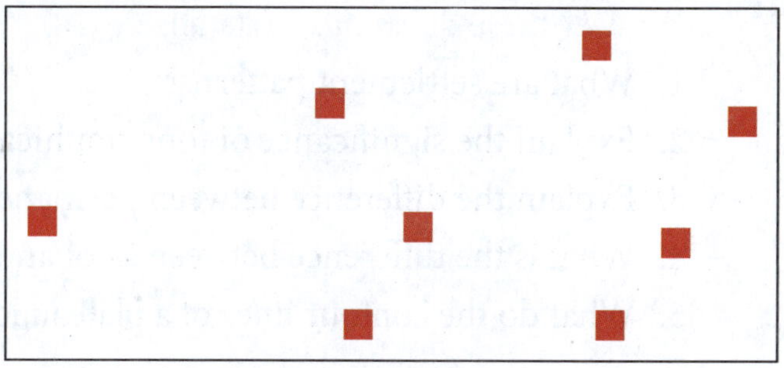

Dispersed settlement

Geo Connect

Making maps or visual references of the world has been an important part of human history. Maps are made to make sense of where we live, make travelling easier or simply learn about a specific region. Detailed maps of India and the South-Asian region have also existed for centuries. David Rumsey, an American map collector, has one of the world's largest private collection of maps. His collections include maps of India dating back to the 18th century based on the survey of the British East India Company. Amongst these is a detailed map of Calcutta made from surveys taken from 1847 to 1849. It shows private and public buildings, temples, aqueducts and ground levels above the tide.

In a Nutshell

- Topographical maps represent a very small area with minute details.
- Contours are imaginary lines joining places with the same heights.
- The distance between two contours is called contour interval.
- A topographical profile depicts the type of landform at a glance.
- The two main types of settlements are temporary and permanent.

Workout

A. Draw the contour diagrams of:

1. Conical hill
2. Plateau
3. Ridge
4. Waterfall
5. Cliff

B. Explain these terms:

1. Contour
2. Triangulated height
3. Bench mark
4. Spot height

C. Answer these questions in detail.

1. What are settlement patterns?
2. Explain the significance of topographical maps.
3. Explain the difference between permanent and temporary settlements.
4. What is the difference between a col and saddle?
5. What do the contour lines of a plateau look like?

Think Box

Topographical maps are very large and often difficult to interpret. Find out how technology has made relief representation easier.

Picture Study

Look at the picture and answer the questions.

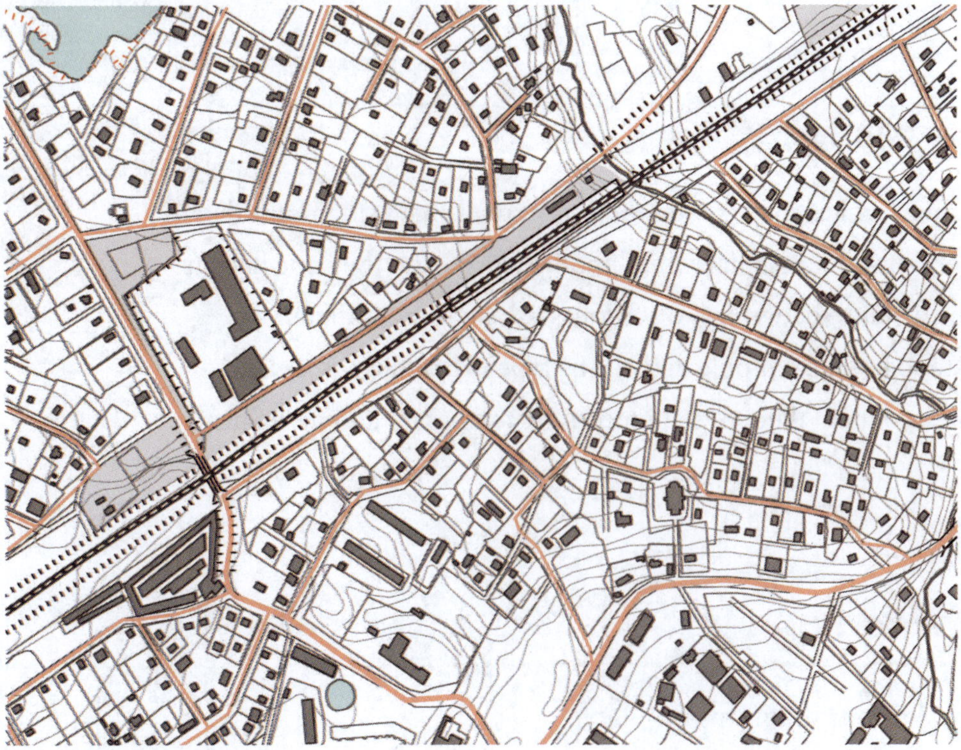

1. What does this map show?
2. How many types of settlements can you identify?

Life Skills and Values

How can we find out information about the cultural features of a place by using a topographical map?

Enjoy

Walk around your neighbourhood and observe the settlement patterns. Draw a map of your neighbourhood and list the types of settlements.

Weblinks

For more information, visit
https://spaceplace.nasa.gov/topomap-clay/en/
Last accessed on 31/July/2020

2 Interpretation of Topographical Maps

Let's learn about...

- interpretation of topographical maps.
- four-figure grid references.
- interpretation of topographical maps.

Key Terms

- topographical sheets
- map interpretation
- grid reference
- drainage
- land use

Reflect

Look at the given contour map and list the landforms you can identify. Does it communicate only relief?

A topographical map or a sheet can be interpreted using the following aspects:

- marginal information
- relief and drainage
- land use pattern
- means of transport and communication
- human settlement

Marginal Information

Marginal information includes the topographical sheet number, its location, grid references, extent in degrees and minutes, scale and districts covered. Topographical maps under the International Map Series of the World are designed to produce standardized maps for the whole world on a scale of 1:10,00,000 and 1:2,50,000.

A sample topographical map

This is how topographical sheets get the number. Toposheet sheet are also known as inch maps.

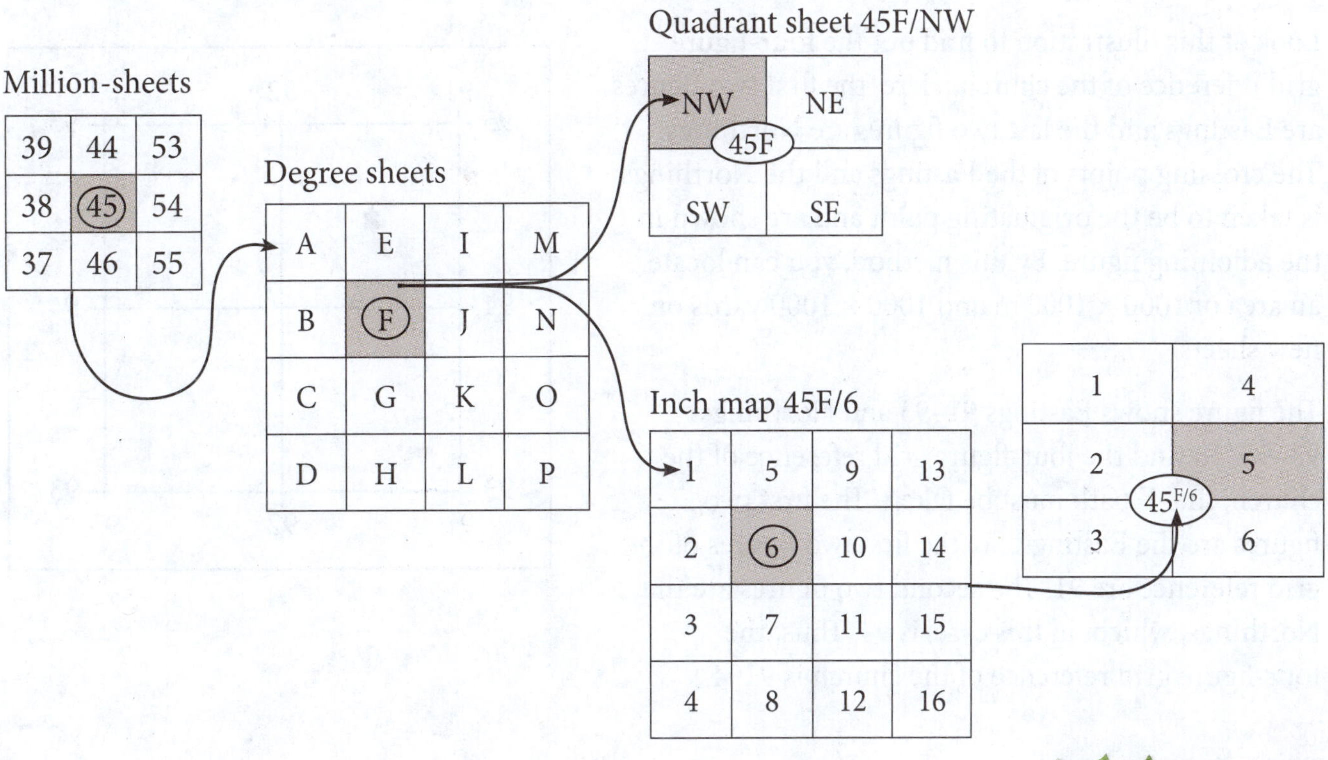

Grid Reference

To interpret topo graphical sheets, you need to understand grid reference. A grid is a set of lines running horizontal and vertical, which help us locate places on a map. You already know that latitudes and longitudes on maps help you locate places. The grid system is also used in topographical sheets.

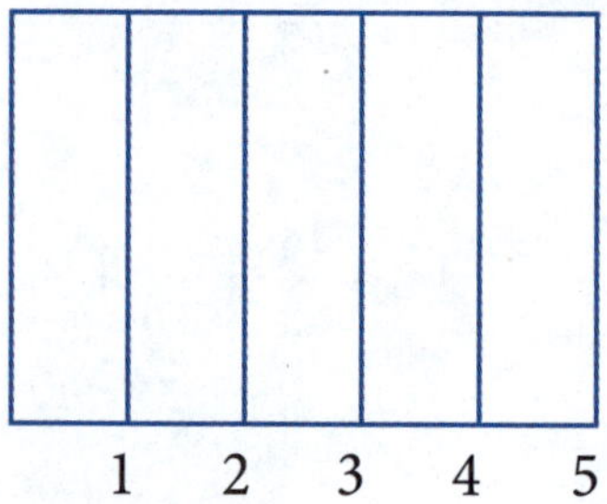

These lines are called **Eastings**, which run from north to south. They indicate the distance east of the origin of the grid reference. The Easting that lies to the left of the object is read. They are always quoted first while giving grid reference.

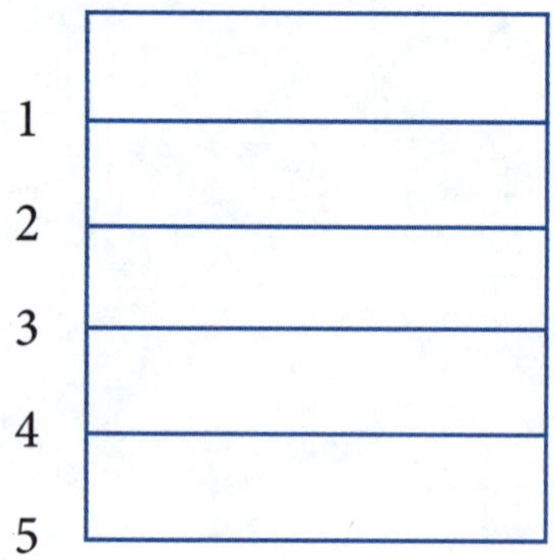

These lines run from east to west and are called **Northings**, since they indicate a distance north of the origin of the grid reference. These lines increase numerically northward and are always quoted after the Eastings. The Northings lie below the object that is to be read.

Four-figure grid reference

Look at this illustration to find out the four-figure grid reference of the church. Here, the first two figures are Eastings and the last two figures are Northings. The crossing points of the Eastings and the Northings is taken to be the originating point and are shown in the adjoining figure. By this method, you can locate an area of 1000 × 1000 m and 1000 × 1000 yards on new sheets.

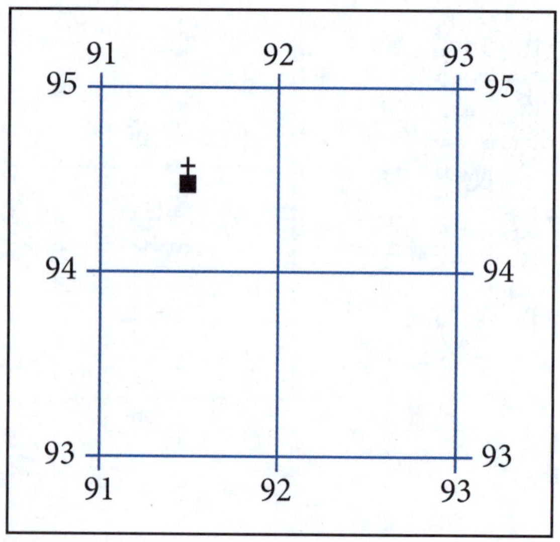

The figure shows Eastings 91–93 and Northings 93–95. To find the four-figure grid reference of the church, the 'L' path must be taken. The first two figures are the Eastings. So, the first two figures of the grid reference are 91. The second two figures are the Northings, which, in this case, is 94. Thus, the four-figure grid reference of the church is 9194.

Relief and Drainage

We have learnt about relief representation in the last chapter. The general topography of the area is studied to identify plains, plateaus, hills or mountains along with peaks, ridges, spurs and the general direction of a slope.

> **Figure Out**
> Which types of drainage patterns does your town have?

A drainage basin is the area drained by a network of rivers and its tributaries. An area drained by a single river is called a catchment area. A drainage system, as seen in the topographical sheets, usually creates a pattern. The three distinct patterns formed are dendritic, trellised and radial.

Dendritic

Dendritic is the most common drainage pattern. It resembles a tree. There is one main river, which is joined by many smaller tributaries. They are mostly formed in places where the river follows the slope of the terrain. Dendritic systems are common in V-shaped valleys.

Trellised

Trellised patterns are rectangular patterns, and tributaries join the main river at right angles. Trellised patterns are found in areas that have alternating hard and soft rock; the stream flows along the bands of soft rock, forming a trellis.

Radial

Radial patterns develop in areas of high topography where elevation drops from a central high area to surrounding low areas.

A. Dendritic pattern develops on relatively uniform bedrock

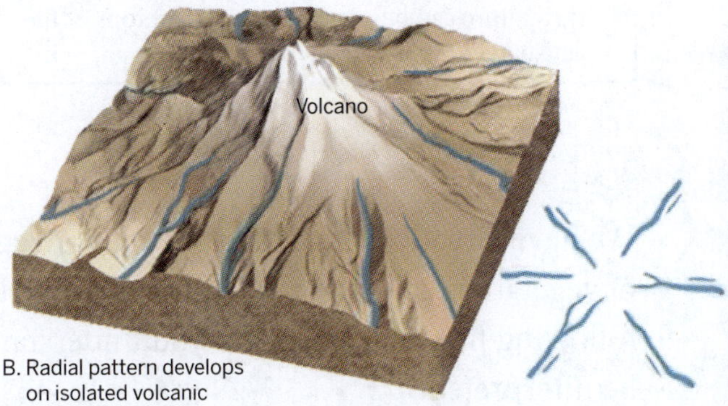

B. Radial pattern develops on isolated volcanic cones or domes

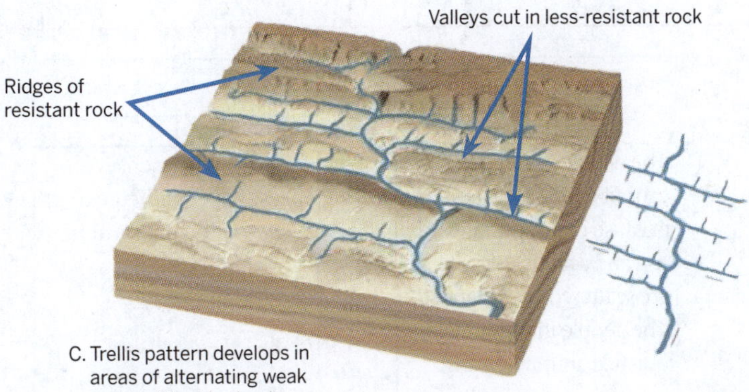

C. Trellis pattern develops in areas of alternating weak and resistant bedrock

trellis: a latticed framework

Land Use Pattern

Relief determines the land use pattern of a place. Land use pattern helps interpret the economic activity of a region. It can be derived from the relief and drainage of the land. The following flowchart will help you understand how to relate the land use pattern with corresponding human activity.

Distribution of Land Use Pattern

Highlands

Mountains, plateaus and glaciated valleys

Note and Study

1. Steepness of the slope
2. Presence of col and saddle
3. Average height
4. Highest point

Inference

- Highlands are unsuitable for agriculture.
- Forestry is an important activity in the highlands.
- Agriculture can be practised on the flat tops of the plateaus.

Lowlands

Gentle slopes with low to average heights

Note and Study

1. Whether the land is gentle or flat
2. The number of rivers and streams
3. The drainage pattern
4. Presence of broken grounds, wells, canals and dams

Inference

- A meandering river indicates a flat gradient, which is suitable for agricultrue.
- Dendritic and trellised drainage patterns are not as suitable for agriculture.
- A disappearing stream indicates sandy soil, which is unsuitable for agriculture.
- A flat lowland is prone to flooding.
- Canals, tubes, tanks and tubewells indicate intensive use of land for agriculture.

Vegetation

We have already learnt that the types of vegetation are related to the climate and the soil. The study of vegetation can also suggest the possible land use pattern and occupation of the people. The following flowchart will help you understand how vegetation cover on a topographical map can be interpreted.

Vegetation

Scattered trees

In lowland areas where agriculture is practised, natural vegetation is cleared. This is indicated by scattered trees.

Scattered scrub land

The desert regions that cannot support agriculture because of poor quality of soil and scarcity of water are scattered scrub lands. The people in these regions practice animal rearing.

Dense forest area

Regions with dense forest cover indicate a region of heavy rainfall.

Open jungle area

Open jungle areas indicate regions that receive moderate rainfall.

DIY

Using topographical maps, find out the drainage patterns of these rivers:

1. Ganga
2. Brahmaputra
3. Indus
4. Periyar
5. Kaveri
6. Kabini
7. Godavari
8. Bhima
9. Beas
10. Jhelum

Transport and Communication Patterns

National highways, state highways, district roads, railways and waterways are means of transportation usually shown on a topographic map. Many maps also show cart tracks, camel tracks and footpaths. Post offices and other communication lines are usually represented using symbols. The means of transport include national or state highways, district roads, cart tracks, camel tracks, footpaths, railways, waterways, major communication lines and post offices. Roads and railways comprise the major transport system on a topographical map. These are influenced the by relief, population, size and resource development pattern of the concerned area. They are indicated with conventional signs and symbols. The means of transport can also help us determine the relief of a place. Road transport is the most favourable mode of transport in regions with hill tracks. A dense network of roads and railways indicate an economically developed area.

Settlement Pattern

We already know about the four types of settlement patterns. The development of towns and villages reflects the use of land and its corresponding economic activity. Mostly, big towns and cities are located in the plains.

The factors that determine the sites of settlements are:

- water
- food
- relief
- occupation
- safety

Human settlement

Settlements near agricultural fields form the productive centres. Settlements near areas of mining and fishing form the extractive centres. Settlements near transport routes form the transport centres, and those near the market form the commercial centres.

Map Interpretation Procedure

Map interpretation involves the study of factors that explain the relationship between several features shown on the map. For example, the distribution of natural vegetation and cultivated land can be better understood if we also have information about settlement and drainage patterns. Similarly, the distribution of settlements can be examined in association with the transport network. The following steps should be followed for interpreting topographical maps.

- Find out the location in India using the index published by the Survey of India. This will give us an idea of the major and minor physiographic divisions of that area. Note the scale of the map and the contour interval; they will provide you the extent and general landform of the area.
- Mark the following features on tracing sheets:

  Major landforms – as shown by contours and other graphical features.

  Drainage and water features – the main river and its important tributaries.

  Land use – forest, agricultural land, wastes, sanctuary, parks, schools, etc.

  Settlement and transport pattern.
- Explain the distribution of each of these features.
- Superimpose the maps and tracing sheets and note down the relationship, if any, between the two patterns. For example, if a contour map is superimposed over a land use map, it provides the relationship between the degree of slope and the type of land use.

Sample Interpretation of Map 45 D/7

Let us interpret a part of the topographical map 45 D/7 given on page 28. This map was published by the Survey of India. This area includes Gujarat and Rajasthan. Let us analyze the topography of this region. An overview of the region is provided to help you interpret the map.

FactPedia

Remote sensing is the use of satellites to collect information about the surface and atmosphere of the Earth. Remote sensing can collect data without making any physical contact with the object. It can detect vegetation, mineral deposits and land use, which are important mapping purposes.

Amazon River through remote sensing

Area

The map covers the districts Banaskantha and Sirohi in Gujarat and Rajasthan, respectively. This region is located in the western region of India on the border between Rajasthan and Gujarat.

Geographical coordinates

Latitude: 24° 15′ N to 24° 30′ N

Longitude: 75° 15′ E to 72° 30′ E

Relief

The relief of the region has few undulations. The area is mainly covered by plains except in the east-central region and the northeastern corner. The slope of the land is from northeast to southwest in the northern part. In the southern part, the land slopes are from east to west. The hills located in the central part have an elevation of about 500 m above mean sea level.

Drainage

The area is drained by two rivers, namely Banas and Sipu Nadi. Sipu Nadi is the tributary of Banas river. The Banas river varies in width and has a narrow perennial course. The dry portion fills in during the monsoon. There are numerous other streams. They rise in the higher ground adjacent to the rivers, and invariably, their courses show large tracts of broken ground indicating soft soil that is easily eroded by water.

Soil

As the area lies in a desert region, it has sandy soil. The area is prone to soil erosion with broken ground near the water course.

Natural vegetation

This region has desert vegetation. The hilly areas have dry deciduous forests with small trees. The plains have scrubs and thorny bushes. Agriculture cannot be practised in this region.

Human settlement

Occupation: We know that the relief of a place determines the land use pattern of a region. Therefore, the main occupation of the people in this region will be animal rearing.

Communication: This region is connected by the Western Railway. Carts are also used for transportation as indicated by the cart tracks on the map.

Settlements: The settlements are small and scattered. They are mainly located in the lowland area. Chitrasani has bigger settlements as it is a rail and road centre. The settlement is nucleated or dispersed in pattern.

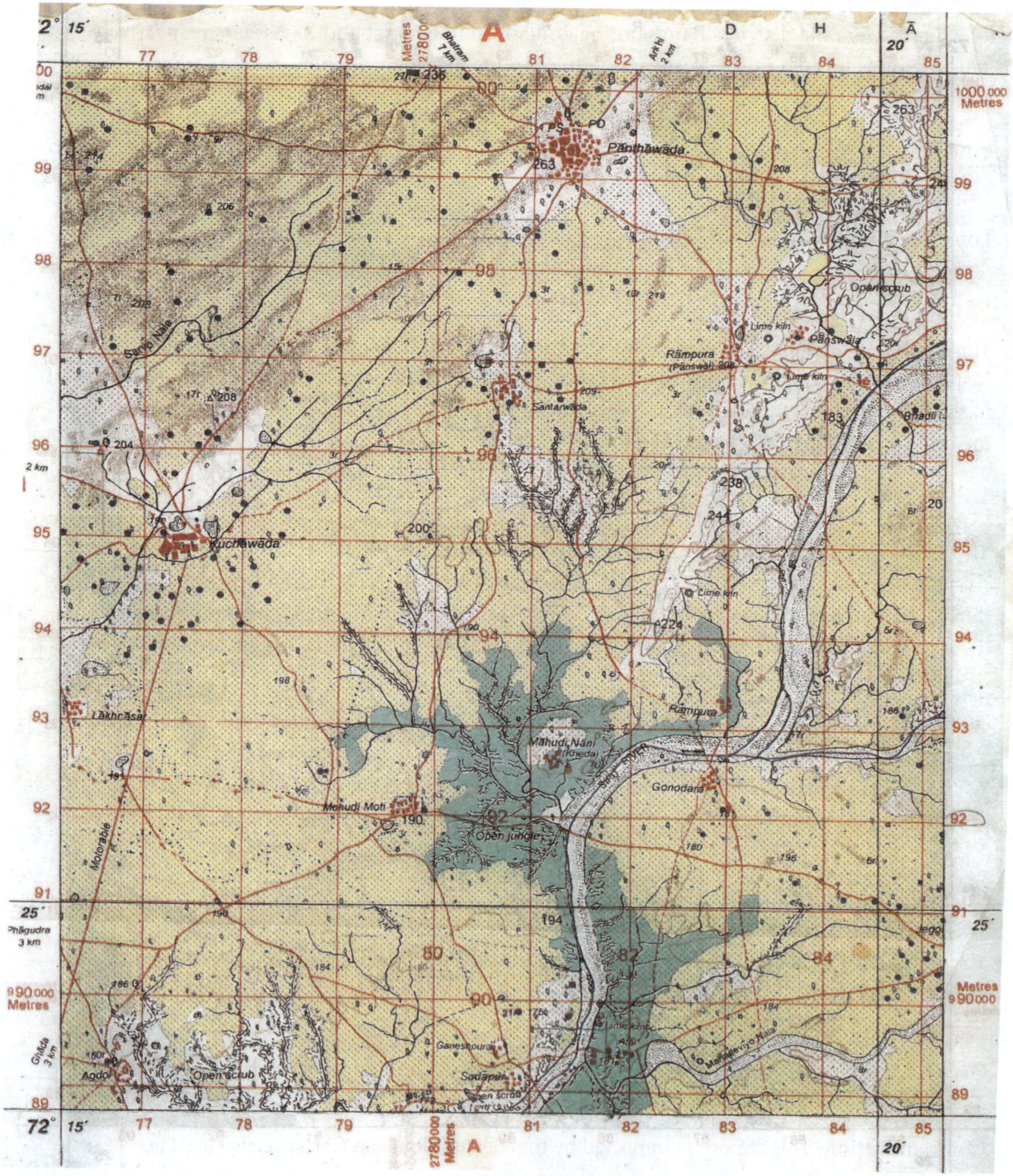

Extract from topographical sheet 45 D/7

Solved Example

1. What is the R.F. of the sheet?

   The R.F. of the sheet is 1:50,000

2. State the four-figure grid reference of:

   a) The Pathwada settlement: 8199

   b) Two lime kilns located in the northeastern side of the map: 8397 or 8396

   c) A temple in the south-west corner: 7688

   d) A dry tank near village Lakhnsar: 7692

   e) The Kuchawada settlement: 7795

   f) The Sodapur village: 8089

3. What does the blue line running through the Sipu river mean?

   The blue line indicates that the river has a narrow channel of water throughout the year.

4. What does ▲ 244 in grid 8294 mean?

   It shows the triangulated height, which means the height of this place is 224 meters above the sea level.

5. Explain the difference between the Sipu river and Mahadeviyo *nala.*

   The Sipu river and the Mahadeviyo river are seasonal rivers. The Mahadeviyo *nala* dries up in the summer, whereas the Sipu river has a narrow channel throughout the year.

6. Where are forests located in this region?

   The forest is located along the Sipu river. The area near the river has the source of both surface and underground water. Hence, it supports forest vegetation.

7. What are the two main occupations of the people in this region?

   The two main occupations of the people in this region are agriculture and forestry. Animal rearing is practised in the patches of open scrub.

8. Which pattern of settlement is found in this area?

   The pattern of settlement found in this area is cluster settlement.

9. Name the drainage pattern in grid 8194.

   The drainage pattern is dendritic.

10. What is the mode of transport used in the region?

    This is a rural area and most of the roads are unmetalled. The refore, the primary means of transport ation is through carts.

Part of Survey of India Topo Map Sheet 45 $\frac{D}{7}$ (Eastings 91-01, Northings 73-83)

Published under the direction of Dr. Prithvish Nag, *Surveyor General of India.* 2003.

Topographical sheet for solved example

In a Nutshell

- A topographical map or a sheet can be interpreted using marginal information, relief and drainage, land use pattern, means of transport and communication and human settlement.
- A grid is a set of lines running horizontal and vertical, which help us locate places on a map.
- To find the four-figure grid reference of the church, the `L' path must be taken.
- Relief determines the land use pattern of a place.
- Map interpretation involves the study of factors that explain the relationship between several features shown on the map.

Workout

A. Look at the topographical map and answer the questions.

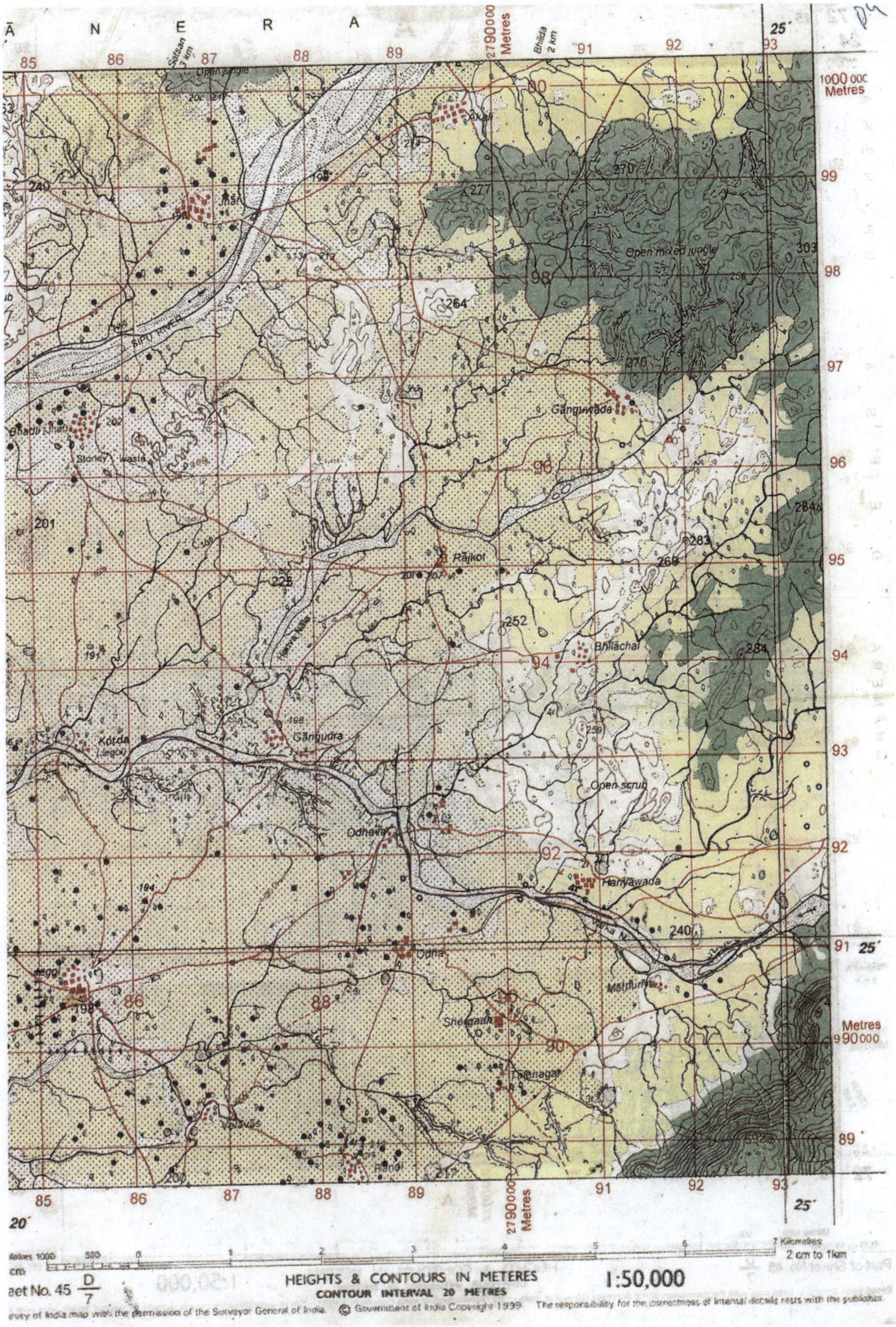

1. What are the two types of scales used besides R.F?
2. What is the contour interval of the given topographical map?
3. Find the four-figure grid references of the following:
   a. Ganguwada village
   b. The temple to the northeast of Odhava
   c. Unlined well to the north of Odhava
   d. Rajkot
   e. ▲217
   f. The island in the Sipu river near the western edge of the map
4. What do the brown dots mean in grid square 8699?
5. What is the general settlement pattern of the region?
6. Explain the drainage pattern of grid 8796.
7. What is the mode of transport in this region?
8. Name the two main occupations of the people of this region. How did you arrive at this conclusion?
9. Name the rivers and *nalas* of the region. Explain the difference between them.
10. Name the man-made features around Jegol (8590).

B. Look at the topographical map and answer the questions.

Part of Survey of India Topo Map Sheet 45 $\frac{D}{7}$ (Eastings 91-01, Northings 90-00)

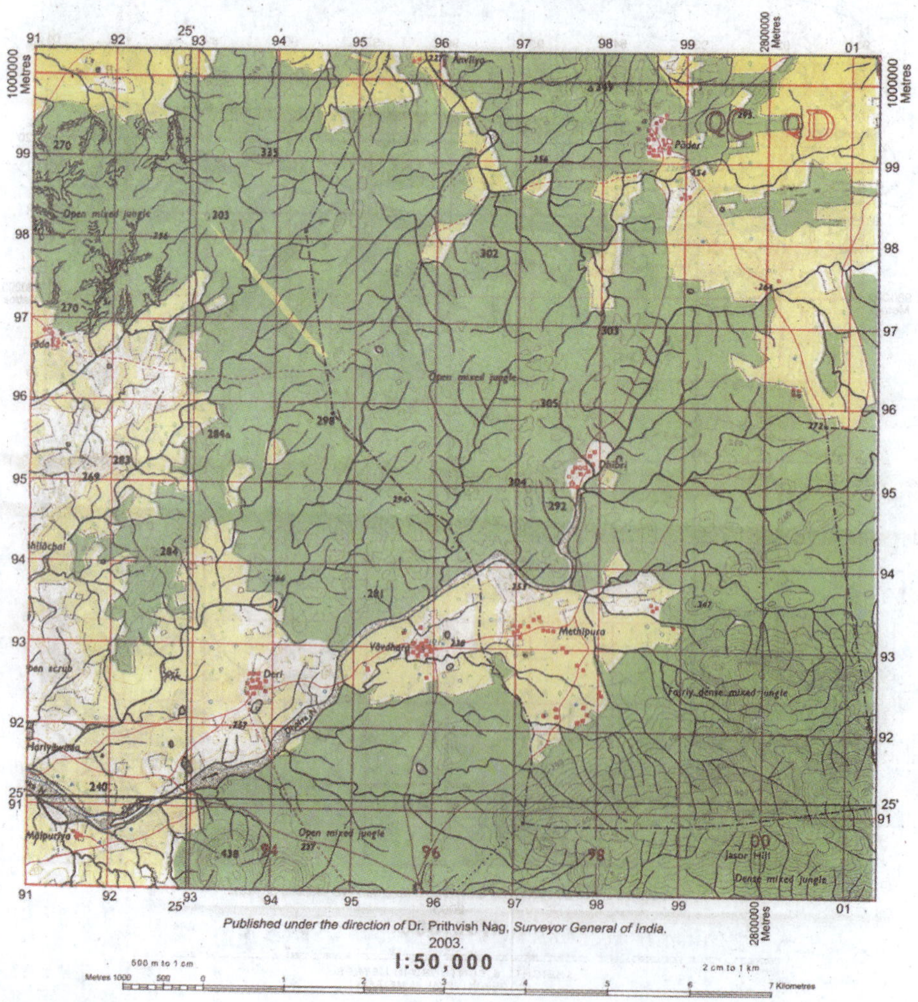

1. Which area is shown in the map?
2. Find out the four-figure grid references of the following:
   a. The well with water near Padar village
   b. Methipura village
   c. ▲ 284
   d. The temple in Dabri village
   e. Dabri village
   f. The highest point of the region
3. What is the drainage pattern of grid 9397?
4. What is the drainage pattern of grid 9489?
5. What is the settlement pattern in grid 9795?
6. Interpret the occupation of the people of this region. Give reasons to support your answer.
7. What is the main mode of irrigation in this region?
8. What type of relief does the southeastern part of the region have?
9. Name the two natural features in grid square 9893.

Think Box

By using a topographical map, find the pattern of rural settlements along the right bank of the river Ganga.

Picture Study

Look at the picture and answer the questions.

1. What do the blue lines represent?
2. What does the dotted red line represent?
3. What do the green patches represent?

Life Skills and Values

How does the drainage pattern of a region affect its settlement pattern?

Enjoy

Make a 3D Contour Model

Things needed: scissors, glue, pen or marker, foam paper

Steps:

1. Choose a contour map of your choice, ideally that of a mountain.
2. Trace and create an outline of the the first layer of elevation.
3. Place the outline of your first layer of elevation on the foam paper and trace the shape of the elevation on the foam paper. Cut this layer out with scissors.
4. Similarly, cut the second line of elevation and stick the first and second layers together.
5. Cut out all the lines of elevation and keep building your model.

Weblinks

For more information, visit
https://www.ncbi.nlm.nih.gov/pmc/articles/PMC5256432/
Last accessed on 31/July/2020

Across the Boundary 1

Make a Knuckle Contour Map

Things needed:

- Water-based or water-soluble markers
- Soap and water for cleaning

Take a look at how contour maps show features of the terrain. Notice that as the elevation of the land increases, a line is made on the map to indicate the shape of the change. Observe how the mountains are depicted with irregular shapes that mark changes in elevation. These shapes appear to be inside each other, like circles within larger circles. Mountain peaks would be the highest, smallest and innermost shapes on maps.

Now that you have reviewed what a contour map is, you can create one on your own.

1. Make a fist with your non-writing hand and place it on a flat surface, knuckles facing up. This will be the terrain for your contour map.
2. Each knuckle will act as a peak of a mountain. Draw contour circles around the surface of the knuckle. First, draw a rough circle around the top of your knuckles since they are the highest points on your hand.
3. Draw a rough circle around the lowest area between your knuckles. Continue to draw lines around the next lowest area as you move from the top of your knuckles to the base of your fist. You can use different colors for each layer of elevation.
4. When finished, flatten out your hand. You now have a two-dimensional contour map of your three-dimensional fist.

Theme 2

Human Geography

Human geography covers a very wide domain and embraces the study of the human race, the movement and growth of population, and different economic activities. It talks about relationships between people and their natural environment.

The study of human and economic geography is vital. It helps us understand cultural and social differences between different groups of people and their relationship with the part of the world in which they live. It also helps us understand the economic activities of people around the world. The way in which natural resources are utilized varies around the world mainly because of population and the level of development of different countries. Uneven distribution of population is closely associated with topographical variations around the globe. In the upcoming chapters, we will study population and human diversity. Another interesting thing that human and economic geography reveals is the way in which every part of the world is interdependent and cannot prosper in isolation.

3 Population Dynamics

Let's learn about...

- distribution of population in the world.
- overpopulation and its effects.
- factors affecting the population of a place.
- composition of population.

Key Terms

- population distribution
- population density
- growth rate
- birth rate
- death rate
- migration
- census

Reflect

Look at the pictures and answer the questions.

1. Which of these places is more crowded? Why?
2. What are the two differences you notice between these places?

Human beings are the biggest consumers of the Earth's resources. Therefore, it is important to know how many people there are in a country, where they live and how and why their numbers are increasing. Population distribution, population density, population growth, population change and characteristics of population are some of the factors that help us understand the population dynamics of a region.

Population Distribution

Population distribution is the spread of people in a particular region. It is the spatial distribution of population shown on a map. There are approximately seven billion people in the world spread unevenly across the globe due to several physical and human factors such as quality of land, climate, availability of natural resources and socio-economic development.

Look at the following population distribution map of the world. A majority of the world's population is concentrated in Asia. It the most populous continent in the world with a population of over four billion people. Almost two billion of this population live in India and China alone.

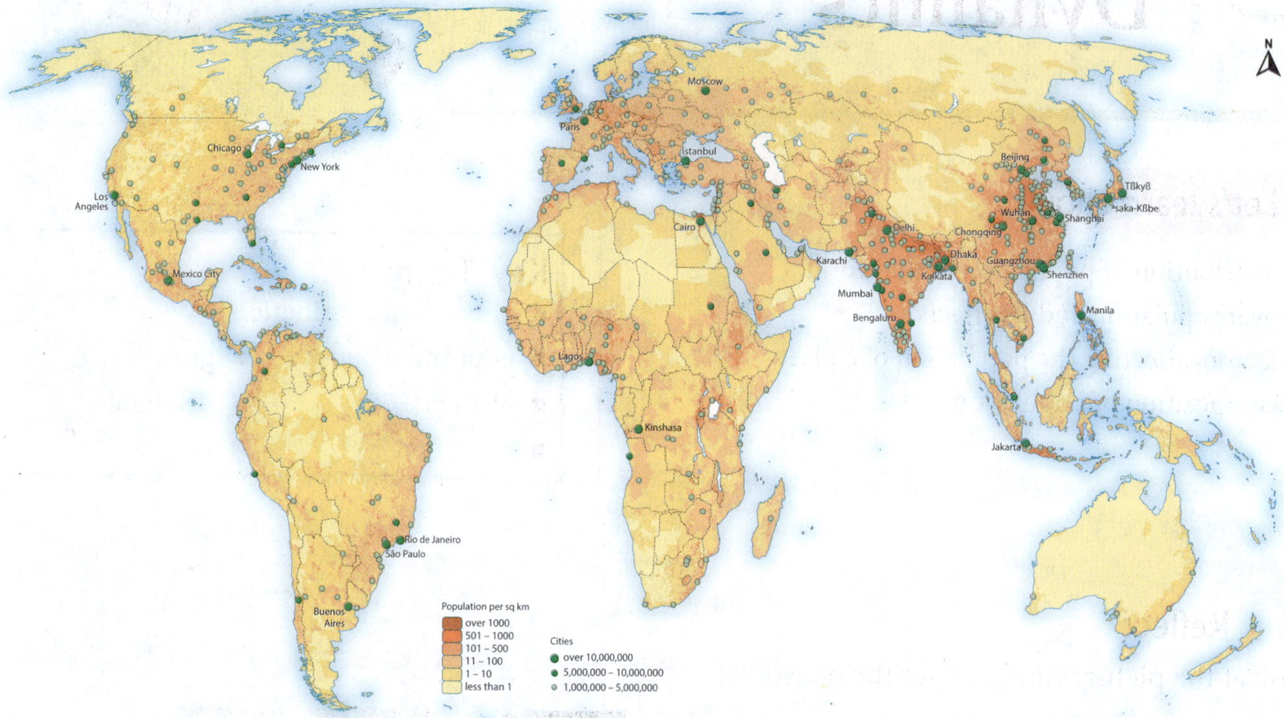

World population distribution

Population Density

Let us a take a look at the world population distribution map again. Beijing, Mumbai, Cairo, New York and Rio de Janeiro each have a population of over 10,000,000 people. These are some densely populated regions of the world. Population density is the number of people per unit area. It provides a better understanding of the spatial distribution of population with relation to land.

Industrial, agricultural and administrative regions are some of the most densely populated places in the world. For example, the Nile River Valley in Egypt, the island of Java in Indonesia, southern Japan, north-eastern United States, western Europe and India are some of the most densely populated regions in the world.

Factors Affecting the Distribution of Population

Let us explore the factors that affect the distribution of population in the world.

Geographical factors

- **Topography:** Plains and plateaus have a higher population compared to mountainous regions. River valleys are densely populated, while mountain regions are sparsely populated.

For example, the land around the Rocky Mountains, the Andes and the Himalayas are sparsely populated compared with the Ganga, the Nile and the Mississippi river valleys. The topography of the plains allows people to lead more comfortable lives, while the rugged topography of hilly regions makes life difficult.

- **Climate:** Regions with extreme climatic conditions are sparsely populated compared with regions with moderate climatic conditions. The tundra and the deserts are the least populated regions in the world. Some examples are the polar regions of Russia, Canada and Antarctica and the desert regions of the Kalahari and the Sahara. The equatorial lowland regions are also sparsely populated because they are hot and wet throughout the year, which makes survival difficult. On the other hand, Southeast Asian countries are densely populated because they have a moderate climate.
- **Water:** Regions with low availability of water are sparsely populated, whereas areas close to water bodies are densely populated. Low availability of water is a major reason for the sparse population in the arid regions of the world. The river valleys are densely populated because water is found in abundance. Cities around the Mississippi river in the United States and the Mackenzie river in Canada are some examples of densely populated regions.
- **Soil and minerals:** The fertility of the soil also affects the distribution of population. The Ganga-Brahmaputra plain in India, the Nile River Valley in Egypt and the basin of the Yangtze river in China are densely populated because these regions have favourable conditions for agriculture. Regions with rich mineral deposits have a developed industry presence that provides employment to people. Hence, these regions are also densely populated. For example, despite scarcity of water and extremely hot temperatures, Saudi Arabia has a considerably higher population than other desert regions in the world.

A settlement along the Nile in Egypt

Socio-economic factors

- The ease of living and social policies of a place also determine its population distribution. Places with affordable living standards have higher population. Basic amenities such as housing, sanitation, healthcare and educational facilities attract a large number of people. Therefore, cities and suburban areas are densely populated, and villages are sparsely populated. London, New York and New Delhi are good examples of such cities.

Green Earth

Expanding cities in developing countries are constructed by clearing forest land thereby putting pressure on transport and water resources.

- The population distribution and density of an area also depend on the type and scale of its economic activities. Factors such as availability of jobs and high wages can contribute to high population density brought about by migration to these areas. Growing commercial activities along with improved transport and infrastructure lead to considerable change in the population distribution of a region. For example, Osaka in Japan, Detroit in North America, Guangzhou in China and Mumbai in India are major economic hubs and hence, are densely populated.

Osaka, Japan

Population Growth

Population growth is the change in the number of people living in a particular region over a period of time. The rate at which the population grows is expressed in percentage. Population growth can be natural or induced. Natural growth in population can be measured by birth and death rates. Induced growth in population is caused by the inflow and outflow, that is, the migration of people. An imbalance in available resources and population makes a country overpopulated. An optimum balance between the population and available resources is important for the overall development of a country.

Impacts of Overpopulation

A large population becomes a burden on the country's economy and resources. Overpopulation may cause the following problems in a region:

- An increase in population leads to increased food demands. When these demands are not met, it causes shortage of food. Shortage of food leads to undernourishment, malnutrition and starvation.
- Land is a precious natural resource. Overpopulation exerts tremendous pressure on the available land. Forests are cleared to make land available for human use, which in turn, affects the environment.
- The main source of water for humans is freshwater bodies. A growing population leads to increased demands for clean drinking water.
- Fossil fuels continue to be the main sources of energy on the Earth today. They are an exhaustible natural resource. The demand for petroleum and natural gas has risen because of an evolving transport system. Energy from fossil fuels is also a basic requirement for households and industries.

Figure Out

What is a population pyramid and what is it used for?

- Due to overpopulation, the consumption of energy increases, while creating pressure on available fossil fuels.

Underpopulation

The average population density of underpopulated countries is low. The polar regions, or countries near the poles, like Greenland, and a few islands on the Pacific Ocean are some examples of underpopulated regions.

It is difficult to increase the population distribution in sparsely populated areas because people are unwilling to forgo modern amenities of towns to settle there. In such places, it is uneconomical to provide and operate an elaborate communication and transportation system. Places with good living conditions attract people, while places with difficult living conditions increase the unwillingness of people to settle there. The disadvantages associated with underpopulation are:

- Underpopulated countries have hostile climatic conditions or relief conditions, which make settlements difficult or dangerous.
- Imbalance between towns and villages is the major problem in underpopulated countries.
- A lack of people makes it difficult for the country to utilize its resources.
- The growth of industries is very slow in such countries as they lack manpower for the workforce.

Population Change

The population of the world is dynamic, that is, it keeps changing constantly in terms of numbers, distribution and composition. In recent years, population has increased drastically. This increase in population reflects the development in agriculture, technology and medical science leading to improved living conditions. The improvement in living conditions has decreased the occurrence of many diseases. There are three main processes that are used to identify the change in population. These are birth rate, death rate and migration.

Birth rate

The term 'birth rate' refers to the number of live births per 1000 people in a year. It is also known as natality. An increase in birth rate leads to an increase in population. For example, if there are 1,450 live births in a place which has a population of 50,000 people, the birth rate can be calculated as:

$$\text{Birth rate} = \frac{\text{number of live births}}{\text{total population}} \times 1000$$

$$\frac{1,450}{50,000} \times 1000 = 29$$

Death rate

The term 'death rate' refers to the number of deaths per 1000 people in a year. Death rate is also referred to as mortality. A decrease in death rate leads to population growth. For example, if there are 450 deaths in a place with a population of 50,000 people, the death rate will be calculated as:

$$\text{Death rate} = \frac{\text{number of deaths}}{\text{total population}} \times 1000$$

$$\frac{450}{50{,}000} \times 1000 = 9$$

The growth rate of a population is the difference between the birth rate and death rate. It is the average annual rate of change in population size during a specified period. It is usually expressed in percentage. Population growth rate measures how fast the size of the population is changing. As long as the birth rate exceeds the growth rate, the population has an ascending trend, that is, the population is increasing.

FactPedia

According to 2013 data, India has an annual population growth rate of 1.2 per cent. China and the United States have annual growth rates of 0.7 and 0.5, respectively.

Migration

Migration is the movement of people from one place to another. It can be internal, that is, within the country, or external, that is, between countries. Migration is an important determinant of population change. It changes not only the population size but also the population composition.

Population Composition

Population composition refers to the structure of the population of a country. It is an important aspect of demographic study as it helps us understand the composition of population defined by characteristics such as gender, age group, education, occupations, place of residence and literacy rate in a particular area.

Age composition

Age composition refers to the number of people in different age groups in a country. The population of a nation is grouped into three broad categories:

- Children (below 15 years)
- Working (15 to 65 years)
- Aged (above 65 years)

The number and percentage of the population within these age groups are notable determinants of the social and economic structure of a population.

A group of school children

Composition of working population

The two broad categories based on a population's working ability are productive population and dependent population. People within the age group of 15–65 years are known as the productive population. These people are employed in primary, secondary or tertiary activities. They are an important index of development and form the main workforce of a country. The dependent population is grouped between 0 to 15 years. They are also called the adolescent population. They are an important human resource for the future and need education and health care.

The productive population is employed in primary, secondary or tertiary activities

Sex ratio

Sex ratio is an important demographic concept. It is defined as the number of females per 1,000 males of the population. It is an important indicator of the equality between males and females in a society.

Rural-urban composition

The rural-urban composition is an indicator of the ratio of people living in rural areas to that of people living in urban areas.

Urban population

The urban population is the population living in urban areas such as cities and towns. A sizeable population in urban areas is an indicator of both development and improved socio-economic conditions. It also indicates an increase in rural-urban migration.

Rural population

The rural population is the population living in villages. Rural areas are important because they provide raw materials for agro-based industries. In recent years, reduced economic activity in rural areas has led to a steady migration of people to urban areas. This phenomenon is called rural depopulation.

Census

The census is the statistical information used to study the population composition of a country. It gives precise information on population, economy, literacy, sex ratio and age composition. The first Census of India was done in 1872. It is revised every ten years. Have you ever noticed people coming to your houses with questionnaires and gathering information about your family members? They have been appointed by the Government of India to collect data which is used in analyzing the population composition.

The census provides accurate data about the population and its demographics

DIY

Study the graph below and answer the questions.

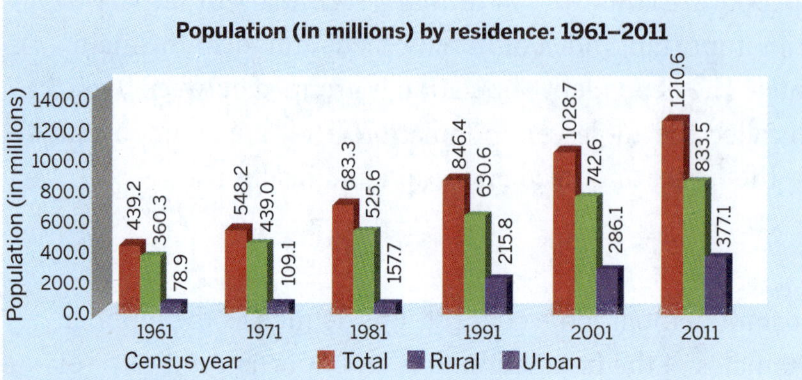

1. In which areas does most of the population of India live?
2. What do you think is the reason for this trend?

Geo Connect

The population of Europe grew slowly and steadily from ancient times until the middle of the 14th century. Between 1347 and 1351, the entire continent was ravaged by bubonic plague, referred to, then, as the Black Death. The Black Death was one of the worst epidemics in the world, which spread from the Far East into Northern Europe. It was transmitted in Europe by the black rat, which acted as a host for the plague. It took around 100 to 150 years for Europe to recover from this epidemic. The previous rate of population growth was resumed only by the end of the 15th century. In the 17th century, the population decreased drastically because of a combination of plague, war and famine. During the 18th century, there was an upward swing in the growth rate of the population, and Europe's population almost doubled between 1700 and 1800. This is usually referred to as population explosion. In the 20th century, the world experienced a sudden and steady growth in population, which reached up to six billion. The main reason for this was better food supplies, medical advancement, decreased death rate and increased birth rate.

In a Nutshell

- Population distribution is the spread of people in a particular region.
- Population density is the number of people per unit area.
- Population growth is the change in the number of people living in a particular region over a period of time.
- The distribution of population on the Earth is affected by various human and geographical factors.
- The numbers, distribution and composition of the population change constantly.

Workout

A. Write T for true and F for false.

1. People below 15 years of age are grouped as children.
2. Migration changes the number, distribution and composition of the population.
3. Asia is the most thinly populated continent in the world.
4. Underpopulation is important for the development of a country.

B. Answer in one word.

1. The number of people living per unit area ....
2. The number of live births per 1000 people per year ....
3. The difference between natality and mortality ....
4. The structure of population in a country ....

C. Fill in the blanks with the correct answers.

1. The people in the .... age group are categorized as the working population.
   a. 15 to 60 b. 15 to 65
   c. 15 to 55 d. 20 to 60
2. .... means the number of females per 1000 males.
   a. Population ratio b. Age ratio
   c. Sex ratio d. Male ratio
3. .... population is an indicator of development and improvement in socio-economic conditions.
   a. Urban b. Rural
   c. Male d. Female
4. The Sahara Desert is sparsely populated because of its ....
   a. favourable climate b. scarce water availability
   c. even terrain d. abundant water bodies
5. The Nile Delta is densely populated because of ....
   a. its hilly terrain b. harsh climatic conditions
   c. availability of fresh water d. less annual rainfall

D. Give reasons.

1. River valleys are densely populated.
2. The Census is an important source of statistical information.
3. A balanced sex ratio is beneficial for a country.
4. Polar regions are the most sparsely populated regions in the world.
5. Migration of people from rural to urban areas.

E. Answer these questions in brief.

1. Discuss the major factors of population growth.
2. Define birth and death rates.
3. Distinguish between population growth and population change.
4. Differentiate between dependent and productive population.

F. Answer these questions in detail.

1. Explain the factors that influence the distribution of population in a region using suitable examples.
2. Discuss the characteristics that determine the composition of the population.
3. What is overpopulation?
4. How are birth and death rates calculated?

G. Map Work

On an outline map of the world, mark the following:

1. Densely populated areas, in red
2. Moderately populated areas, in yellow
3. Sparsely populated areas, in green

Think Box

What are the significant features of the National Population Policy launched by the Government of India in 2000?

Picture Study

Look at the picture and answer these questions.

1. Who do you think is the dependent population in this picture?
2. Is the teacher a part of the dependent or productive population?

Life Skills and Values

Conduct research about the family welfare schemes in India. Mention how they are important for the development of a nation.

Enjoy

Make a PowerPoint presentation on the factors that have contributed to the growth of population in the developing countries of the world.

Weblinks

For more information, visit
https://www.un.org/en/sections/issues-depth/population/index.html
Last accessed on 31/July/2020

4 Migration

Let's learn about...

- migration.
- types of migration.
- causes of migration.
- impacts of migration.
- brain drain caused by migration.

Key Terms

- migration
- brain drain
- population
- rural
- urban
- immigration
- emigration

Reflect

Read the passage and answer the questions.

Bheem and his wife Poonam live in a small village in Uttar Pradesh. The nearest city is Lucknow, which is about 1000 km away. Bheem and Poonam do not own any land. They do odd jobs for big farmers to make a living. Their income is not steady as the jobs they do are temporary. Often, Bheem gets ₹50 for a day's hard work but most of the time, he is paid in kind. Managing two meals a day becomes impossible for Bheem and Poonam. Providing education to their children is extremely difficult. To access healthcare, Bheem had to leave his village and go to Lucknow, which has hospitals. Bheem managed to get a job there as a daily wage labourer in a sugar factory. His daily income has increased to at least ₹200 per day. Bheem's family continues to live in the village but he plans to bring his wife, Poonam, and their children to the city to provide them with a better standard of living.

1. Why did Bheem and Poonam leave the village?
2. Do you think their life is more comfortable in Lucknow than in the village? If yes, why?

Have you ever wondered why people migrate to other places? Migration of people can arise out of social, economic or political reasons. Before we study further about the reasons for migration, let us find out more about what it means.

Defining Migration

Migration is the inflow or outflow of people from one place to another. People change their residential location for reasons that may be voluntary or involuntary or a combination of both. The movement of people from one place to another influences the population of a region. People may move within the country or from one country to another.

Types of Migration

Migration is of two types—internal and external.

Internal migration

Moving to a new residence within a state or a country is called internal migration. Internal migration is of two types: rural to urban migration and urban to urban migration.

Rural to urban migration: Rural to urban migration is the movement of people from rural areas to urban areas. This is caused by a number of factors such as employment opportunities, marriage, better wages and better social and civic amenities. People living in villages often engage in jobs in the unorganized sector. These are mostly contract jobs such as those of labourers and farmers. In cities, people working in the unorganized sector find jobs which provide security and a steady income. In big cities, you will find small jhuggis made by rural migrants. Education is also an important factor that causes rural to urban migration. Young people often migrate to cities to avail quality education.

People in overloaded rickshaws on a highway near Agra

Urban to urban migration: Urban to urban migration is the movement of people from one urban region to another. People move to new urban areas known as a new town or an overspill town. A new town is a planned urban centre created in a rural area with the government's aid. Navi Mumbai in Mumbai, Lavasa in Pune and New Town in Kolkata are some examples of new towns. An overspill town is a town that is established to house the excess population of a nearby city. These are also called satellite towns. Manesar, Noida and Gurugram are examples of overspill towns.

An urban township

In developing countries like India, migration can be explained by the flowchart given below.

Villages → **Local small towns** → **Big cities**

People first migrate from villages or rural areas to local towns. From local small towns, they migrate to urban regions, that is, big cities. Urban migration is one of the major reasons for urban sprawl or rapid expansion of urban areas. Population growth, industrialization, lack of affordable housing, demand for more living space and transportation are some of the main reasons for urban to urban migration.

jhuggis: a slum dwelling typically made of mud and corrugated iron; urban sprawl: the uncontrolled expansion of urban areas

External migration

External migration may be defined as the movement or change of the place of residence from one country to another. This change of residence can be permanent or extended over a long period of time. Most of the time, external migration takes place in a sequence of events within a family or a certain group of people. This is called **chain migration**. **Chain migration** often begins with the relocation of a single family member who then brings other family members to the new location. The clustering of people from a specific region into certain neighbourhoods or small towns is a direct consequence of chain migration. The causes of external migration can be economic, political or familial. Natural causes such as earthquakes and droughts are also responsible for external migration. Economic conditions are major reasons of external migration. International and regional conflicts, civil wars and poverty also lead to migration of people from one country to another.

Person A migrates alone for a job overseas → **Spouse, children and other family members join Person A** → **Once the migrant worker settles in the new country, other community members follow the same pattern**

When a person leaves the country of residence and moves to another country, it is called **emigration**. For example, Sudan and Jamaica have experienced a decrease in population due to emigration. When a person enters a new country, it is called **immigration**. **Immigrants** are people who move from their native country to a new country. Countries such as Australia and Canada have a large immigrant population.

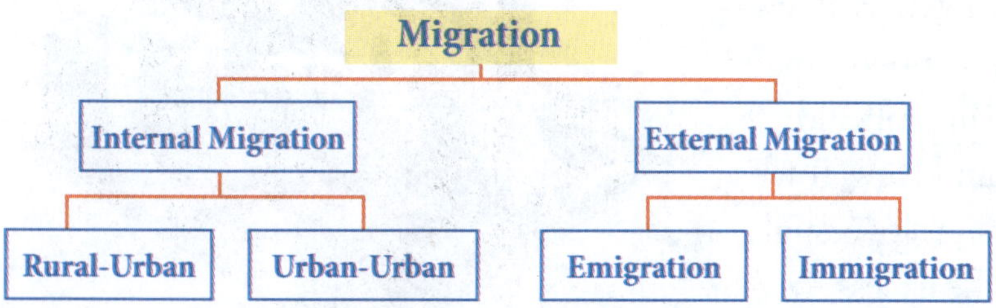

Types of migration

Figure Out

Which countries support immigration and why?

People queue at an immigration counter

DIY

Read the passage and answer the questions.

Bedford in the United Kingdom has a huge Italian community that migrated from southern Italy after the Second World War. Italians make up about one-fifth of the population. After the devastating war, there was a dearth of jobs and Italian workers migrated to Bedford to work in brick factories. They also brought their families with them. As their wages improved, they bought houses and started trading goods. They also procured British citizenships for their families. Most of the people in Bedford migrated because they knew someone in Bedford.

1. Why did the workers come to Bedford from Italy?
2. Which type of migration took place in Bedford?

Causes of Migration

Migration is caused by many reasons, categorized as push and pull factors. Push factors are living conditions of people at the original place. These are the reasons why people move out of a particular geographical region. Pull factors are the conditions or circumstances of the new place that attract people to settle there. Poverty and lack of employment opportunities are examples of push factors. Better infrastructure and educational institutions are examples of pull factors.

Let us read about a few causes of migration.

Geographical causes

People often migrate because of geographical reasons such as unavailability of fertile land and harsh terrain. Have you heard about the Magyar tribes? They were people who once lived in the mountainous regions of the Urals in Russia until they migrated to present-day Hungary. Many agricultural communities who could not make a living in their own country because of shortage of land or infertile land migrated to regions that had fertile land. The 19th century witnessed many such migrations. European farmers migrated to the United States of America, Australia, New Zealand and South America in search of farms or huge plots of land for cultivation because they were landless peasants.

Economic causes

Unemployment is one of the most important reasons why people migrate to different places within their country or travel overseas. Workers also move to other countries to earn more. People move to more developed industrial countries in search of jobs that provide higher wages.

Poverty often drives people to seek work in cities

Political causes

Throughout history, and even in recent years, we have seen people move out of their countries due to political unrest or political persecution. The First World War and the Second World War also caused the migration of numerous people. The Indian subcontinent witnessed a huge migration during the Partition of India. Refugees, either from war or conflict zones or from politically oppressed regions, are also forced to migrate to safer regions to save their lives. Currently, a large number of people from Syria have taken refuge in Turkey.

FactPedia

A large number Indians worked on sugar plantations in Fiji, Mauritius, and the West Indies, especially in Trinidad and Guyana. Indians also went to East Africa where they were engaged mainly in trade. The eminent writer and Nobel laureate, V. S. Naipaul, has provided a vivid account of migrant Indian workers in his novel, *Half A Life*.

persecution: hostility or ill-treatment

Impacts of Migration

We know that migration occurs because of certain push and pull factors. People move out of places that lack opportunities and resources. The impact of the movement of population is very significant and changes a region economically, socially, culturally, politically and demographically. Migration has both positive and negative consequences. Let us find out more about the impacts of migration.

Economic impacts

When migration takes place, it affects both the region of origin and the region to which people migrate. Reduced unemployment in the region of origin is one of the positive outcomes of migration. Immigration impacts the human resources of the region. New skills and talent are a boost to the economy of a region. When people migrate, they send money to their families. This money is called remittance. Remittance is an important source of foreign exchange for a country. Remittance received from external migration of people plays an important role in the growth of the economy of the source area. Most of this money is reused for education, agriculture and construction purposes. Internal migrants also bring in remittances, but these are meagre. Migration of people decreases the shortage of labour. Skilled labour from different countries can be very beneficial for the economy.

Social impacts

Social change is an inevitable outcome of migration. Migration leads to the intermixing of people of diverse cultures. This is beneficial for a society as ideas and thoughts from different cultures creates a broader outlook among people. The acceptance of migrants by native people is an issue that can bring about a positive or a negative change in the society. Sometimes, migrants face rejection within the society, which in turn gives rise to other social evils.

Demographic impacts

Migration causes the redistribution of population and changes the demography of a region. Internal migration leads to the expansion of towns and cities. Urban sprawl is a direct consequence of internal migration. External migration leads to depopulation, especially in developing regions. Migration increases the population of developed nations. Countries such as the United States, Australia and New Zealand have a huge migrant population.

Chowpatty Beach on Marine Drive in southern Mumbai has experienced urban sprawl

Environmental impacts

Environmental deterioration is probably the biggest negative aspect of migration. Migration causes overcrowding of urban regions. This puts tremendous pressure on the resources and infrastructure of a place. Over-exploitation of natural resources, such as fossil fuels, also affects the environment adversely.

foreign exchange: currencies of other countries

Migration and the World

The United States of America

The United States of America, which has the highest number of immigrants in the world, has witnessed two of the biggest human migrations worldwide. Historically, migration in America can be divided into the Great Migration that occurred between 1916 and 1970 and the Second Great Migration that occurred between 1940 and 1970. During the Great Migration, approximately six million African-Americans migrated from the predominantly rural southern United States to the urban regions, which include the west, mid-west and the northeast United States. The Great Migration occurred because of social, political and economic reasons. The social segregation of African-Americans and the lack of social and economic opportunities led to this migration. The Second Great Migration was larger in scale and was the result of the lack of jobs and racial discrimination.

Latin America

During the 19th and 20th centuries, the southern regions of South America saw a large influx of migrants. Colonists from Spain and Portugal populated Argentina, Uruguay and Brazil.

Recent years

The world migration pattern has been showing a changing trend. The recent migration trend shows people from developing nations moving to developed nations like the United States, Canada and Britain. It also shows the movement of whole families in search of new opportunities. Migration contributes to inclusive and sustainable economic growth and development in both the home and the host country. The funds sent by immigrants are often used to improve the livelihoods of families and communities in the home countries. The money is invested in education, health, sanitation and housing. These migrants fulfil the critical shortage of labour and also contribute to the growth of the host countries.

FactPedia

In 2015, India had the largest diaspora in the world (16 million), followed by Mexico. Other countries with large diasporas included Russia, China, Bangladesh, Pakistan and Ukraine.

Brain Drain

One aspect of external migration in modern times is the movement of highly qualified or skilled people. In recent years, skilled workers have moved to foreign countries for better salaries and jobs. They could have been employed in their native countries; however, better opportunities and higher standards of living act as pull factors causing their migration. A considerable number of software engineers, management professionals, medical practitioners and teachers migrate to the Middle East, the United Kingdom, Canada and the United States for jobs. This type of migration is called 'brain drain' as it takes away a chunk of well-qualified human resources who are valuable to the source country. Brain drain is a major concern for developing countries like India. Over the years, many skilled and talented young people from India have moved to western countries, primarily Europe and the United States.

diaspora: people living outside their native country

Impact

Brain drain can weaken the economies of developing countries by depriving these countries of skills that can help in the country's overall growth and development. However, the host country may benefit from brain drain in the form of skilled labour and workforce, while the country of origin can benefit from remittances.

Geo Connect

The Indian immigration to the United States began in the late 1960s. The migration was triggered by the dearth of jobs in India and the need for technical expertise, scientists and engineers in the United States. This favoured India, which had a considerable number of trained manpower that struggled with opportunities for employment within India. Most of these Indian immigrants comprised fresh and talented graduates from premier educational institutes in India. Many Indians started working in the Silicon Valley in California, which has a huge information technology industry. Although they form only a small part of the total population of the United States, Indian Americans are a rapidly growing group of people in the world.

In a Nutshell

- The movement of people from one place to another is called migration.
- There are two kinds of migration–internal migration and external migration.
- Internal migration leads to the development of towns and cities.
- External migration leads to depopulation.

Workout

A. Fill in the blanks with the correct answers.

1. People in villages are engaged in the .... sector.

   a. organized b. industrial c. public d. unorganized

2. .... migration leads to depopulation in the areas around the cities.

   a. Internal b. External c. Rural to rural d. Urban to urban

3. Migrating from one's home country to a new country is called ....

   a. brain drain b. internal migration

   c. external migration d. emigration

4. .... is the money sent by the migrants to the source country.

a. Remittance
b. Foreign exchange
c. Service tax
d. Loans

B. Write T for true and F for false.

1. Push factors are living conditions of people at the original place. ☐
2. Unemployment is one of the major causes for international migration. ☐
3. Migration always has a positive impact on society. ☐
4. Urban sprawl increases due to internal migration. ☐

C. Answer these questions in brief.

1. Explain the geographical factors that cause human migration.
2. Differentiate between external and internal migration.
3. What are the two types of internal migration?
4. How are overpopulation and underpopulation related to migration?
5. What is brain drain?

D. Answer these questions in detail.

1. Explain the push and pull factors of migration.
2. What are the causes of rural to urban migration?
3. How does migration cause urban sprawl?
4. Explain the impacts of migration.

Think Box

It is believed that the earliest humans originated from Africa and migrated to different parts of the world. Research on the Internet and review some of the causes of ancient human migrations. How do you think they differ from modern reasons for migration?

Picture Study

Look at the picture and answer these questions.

1. This is a group of people moving to another place. What are they called?
2. Name two countries from which people have been moving out rapidly.

Life Skills and Values

In your neighbourhood, talk to people who have migrated from nearby villages, other cities or even different countries. Make a list of the reasons for the migration and categorize them as push or pull factors.

Enjoy

Write a script for a street play to explain the merits and demerits of migration.

Weblinks

For more information, visit
http://www.bbc.co.uk/education/guides/zkg82hv/revision/5
Last accessed on 31/July/2020

5 Urbanization

Let's learn about...

- urbanization.
- causes of urbanization.
- effects of urbanization.
- smart cities.

Key Terms

- cities
- population
- urbanization
- smart cities
- urban sprawl

Reflect

Look at the images and answer the questions.

1. What difference do you notice between these places?
2. Where do you think most people would like to stay and why?
3. Name a few activities people might be engaged in the first picture.

Urbanization is a process by which people living in predominantly rural areas move to towns and cities. It involves expansion of urban places or an increase in the size of existing cities. However, growth of population is only one aspect of urbanization. It also includes modernization and social change. Urbanization can also be understood as an increase in the proportion of people living in urban areas compared with rural areas. It is also called urban sprawl.

Mumbai, India

History of Urbanization

Urbanization is not a recent phenomenon. Its history can be traced back to the period when human beings started practising farming and leading settled lives. They moved to regions that had fertile soil and a warm and rainy climate. With the domestication of animals and innovations in the methods of irrigation, human settlements expanded and villages came into existence. The invention of the wheel revolutionized the transport system, enabling humans to move from one place to another easily. This also allowed humans to socialize and trade goods.

Causes of Urbanization

Population growth

Population growth is one of the main causes of urbanization. The growth in population can be natural, that is, it may be caused by an increased birth rate or migration. You have already learnt that people migrate from rural areas to urban areas for better jobs and living conditions. As a result, urban areas such as towns and cities expand causing rapid urbanization.

Industrialization

The transition of a non-industrial region to an industrial one is also one of the causes of urbanization. The establishment of industries creates new jobs in cities. As a result, unemployed people from villages move to cities in search of jobs. The mechanization of farms in villages causes loss of jobs to farmers who move to urban areas to work and make a living. Developing countries are currently going through a phase of rapid industrialization. Therefore, the rate of urbanization is higher in developing countries and lesser in developed countries.

Rural-urban transformation

An increase in the income and number of working people creates a demand for new or more housing space for individuals. This encourages developers to rapidly construct new houses. The rapid development of housing and other urban infrastructure causes uncontrolled urban expansion.

Noida, Uttar Pradesh

Employment opportunities

Urban centres provide better employment opportunities. When agricultural income becomes low, people from rural regions migrate to urban centres. The prospects of a job in the organized sector and job security draws people from rural to urban areas.

Education

People from rural regions seek admission in educational institutes in urban regions that generally provide better education. Consequently, educational institutes have started mushrooming in cities to accommodate these students. This leads to urbanization.

A group of school children in a rural area

mushrooming: to increase drastically in number

FactPedia

Paris is considered to be one of the best cities in the world. It is an important trading centre, a confluence zone of art and culture and an important administrative centre. However, Paris was not always like this. Paris was an island located on the river Seine. Building a bridge across the Seine transformed the city. Its location on the converging routes made it a trading centre and gave it the strategic importance that it enjoys till today. Thus, the central location of Paris made it one of the most important administrative cities of the world.

Standard of living

Generally, living and property costs are higher in the city than in the countryside. This encourages countryside development. A majority of urban residents seek to settle within the core city, but the lower costs of living and property attract them to the countryside. This causes urbanization of the countryside or suburban regions.

Figure Out

Trace the development of Jamshedpur, Bhilai and Durgapur as manufacturing centres.

Transportation

Transportation routes provide easy access to urban centres. The construction of expressways and highways cause congestion in the city. Roads are commonly considered a major catalyst of urban sprawl. The development of the urban economy and job opportunities are directly dependent on transportation facilities.

Impacts of Urbanization

Urbanization may have both positive and negative impacts. However, its negative impacts are generally more pronounced because urbanization is often uncontrolled. The consequences of urbanization can be evaluated based on its socio-economic and environmental effects. Often these overlap or may have several indirect impacts. The major consequences of urbanization are as follows:

Higher living costs

Urbanization leads to an increase in living costs. Overpopulation leads to an increase in the demand of public services and for the maintenance and improvement of urban infrastructures such as fire stations, police stations, schools, hospitals, roads, drinking water and sanitation. Therefore, the cost at which these services are available also increases.

London is one of the most expensive cities in the world

catalyst: a thing that increases the rate at which an event occurs

Traffic congestion

Urbanization increases traffic flow from the suburbs to the central city, leading to more fuel consumption. This causes traffic congestion. More cars on roads covering greater distances cause traffic gridlock.

Ghetto and slums in Delhi, India

Impact on wildlife and ecosystem

An increase in the population of a region may lead to an alteration of ecosystems. Development associated with urbanization decreases the amount of forest area, farmland and open space. The spread of urban sprawl into rural natural areas such as forests and wetlands is one of the primary reasons for wildlife habitat loss. Roads, power lines and pipelines often pass through natural areas or fragmenting forests. The fragmentation of a large forest into smaller patches disrupts the ecological balance and reduces the availability of habitats for some species. Some forest fragments are too small to maintain a viable population of certain wildlife species.

Poor air quality

Urbanization is often cited as the main cause of air pollution. It leads to an increase in fossil fuel consumption and emission of greenhouse gases. Increased use of automobiles adds more air pollutants such as carbon monoxide, carbon dioxide, sulphur dioxide, nitrogen oxides and microscopic particles in the atmosphere. These pollutants can affect plant growth, create smog and acid rain, contribute to global warming and cause serious health problems.

Beijing has poor air quality

Water pollution

Urbanization has a serious impact on water resources. Rainwater does not soak into the ground because of increased urban construction, and groundwater aquifers are not replenished. Urban growth and sprawl has led to an increase in the volume of total surface runoff. Therefore, urban areas are exposed to increased flood hazard, inundation and erosion, which in turn leads to an increase in water pollution from runoff contaminated with garden chemicals and motor oil. Pollutants are consumed by humans when they eat contaminated fish from affected water bodies and when they drink from contaminated surface water or groundwater sources.

suburbs: residential areas located in the outskirts of a city; traffic gridlock: when vehicles move uncontrollably from all directions and cause traffic jams; viable: capable of surviving

Smart Cities

Singapore is one of the best smart cities in the world

We know that that cities are a benchmark of development but at the same time, they face challenges related to a growing population, which in turn leads to multiple problems. Countries all over the world are trying to find a solution to these problems. In order to combat the negative effects of urbanization, smart cities are being set up in most developing nations of the world.

Smart cities provide core infrastructure, a decent quality of life and a clean and sustainable environment.

Smart cities are expected to reduce the problems related to urban centres such as water scarcity, traffic congestion and unplanned growth.

Smart cities have the following.

- Adequate supply of clean drinking water
- Assured electricity provision and eco-friendly solar panels for streetlights and lights in parking areas
- Efficient sanitation and garbage disposal facilities to keep the city clean and hygienic
- Special safety measures and parks for old people and children
- Eco-friendly surroundings to protect the environment
- Well-planned traffic flow to avoid traffic congestion during the busy hours of the day
- Free Wi-Fi zones for easy communication
- Efficient waste management

Barcelona

Efforts at the Local Level

Municipalities in small towns and corporations of big urban centres play a significant role in keeping the city clean.

- They provide regular supply of clean drinking water.
- They take care of the environment by careful disposal of solid waste and proper sanitation.
- They are responsible for enabling easy transportation and communication within the city.
- Construction on roads and flyovers for organized traffic flow within urban areas and avoid traffic congestion is also a responsibility of municipalities.

benchmark: a standard or a reference point

- They plan the use of available land properly and effectively.
- They help preserve open spaces for parks, gardens and tree plantations.
- Mapping of residential, industrial and administrative areas and marketplaces within the demarcated urban area is another responsibility of municipalities..

DIY

Study the table and answer the questions.

JNNURM Projects – Sector-wise sanction (Urban Infrastructure and Governance)

S. No.	Sector	Number of Projects Sanctioned	Cost of Projects Sanctioned (Million)
1	Water Supply	140	1,82,346
2	Sewerage	99	1, 21,167
3	Drainage/Storm Water Drainage	59	72,888
4	Solid Waste Management	40	21,861
5	Roads/Flyovers	75	33,822
6	Public Transport System	19	47,709
7	Other Urban Transport	13	6,860
8	Urban Renewal	9	4,451
9	Development of Heritage Areas	2	492
10	Preservation of Water Bodies	4	1,167
11.	Parking	1	560
Total		461	4, 94,224

Source: JNNURM, Progress Review, April 24, 2009

1. What are the concerned areas for the local government of this urban centre?
2. Which are the greatest and the least area of concerns for the local government?
3. Why do you think the development of heritage areas is included in the list?
4. Why should there be areas demarcated for parking? How is this helpful to people?

Geo Connect

Brazil has experienced massive urbanization. Many developing countries are currently in the process of urban development. However, Brazil experienced urbanization much earlier compared with other Latin American countries. Brazil also faces problems related to the outlining areas of the cities. Sao Paulo is the country's economic centre. Brazil's modern administrative, financial, educational and cultural services are concentrated in this city.

In a Nutshell

- Urbanization is a process by which people start living in towns and cities instead of living in predominantly rural areas.
- Population growth is one of the main reasons behind urbanization. Industrialization, rural-urban transformation, employment opportunities, education, standard of living and transportation are the other causes of urbanization.
- Urbanization leads to higher living costs, traffic congestion, impact of wildlife and ecosystem, poor air quality and water pollution.
- The consequences and significance of urbanization can be evaluated based on its socio-economic and environmental effects.
- Smart cities provide core infrastructure, a decent quality of life and a clean and sustainable environment.
- Municipalities in small towns and corporations of big urban centres play a significant role in keeping the city clean.

Workout

A. Answer in one word.

1. An increase in the proportion of people living in urban areas compared with rural areas ....
2. Cities that provide core infrastructure, a decent quality of life and a clean and sustainable environment. ....
3. Process by which people from rural areas move to towns and cities ....

B. Give reasons for the following.

1. Urbanization is necessary for human development.
2. Urban suburbs are now becoming a common sight.
3. People prefer to live in cities than villages.
4. Smart city projects will combat the effects of urbanization.

C. Answer these questions in brief.

1. What do you understand by the term urbanization?
2. What does mechanization of farms in villages lead to?
3. What is urban sprawl?
4. Explain the term smart city.

D. Answer these questions in detail.

1. What are the main the reasons for rapid urbanization?
2. How does the government help keep cities clean?
3. What do you mean by smart cities? State some of the features of smart cities.
4. What are the impacts of urbanization?

Think Box

Study the table and answer the questions.

Population of India	
TOTAL	1,210,193,422
RURAL	833,087,662
URBAN	377,105,760

1. Where do you think more people stay in India?
2. What is the percentage difference between the people living in rural areas and the people living in urban areas?
3. Why do you think the population is more in the rural sector?

Picture Study

Look at the picture and answer the questions.

1. This a picture of Mumbai. Why do you think Mumbai is densely populated?
2. What problems does Mumbai face because of population explosion?

Life Skills and Values

Classify these places into manufacturing centres, educational centres, entertainment centres, religious centres and defensive centres.

a. Berlin
b. Rome
c. Nova Scotia
d. Ramoji Film City
e. Jamshedpur
f. Cambridge

Enjoy

Develop a plan for a smart city with a population of 10,500 people and these features:

a. A residential area
b. City malls
c. Town halls and community halls
d. Roads and bridges
e. Parks

Calculate the total area of the smart city and provide enough space for each feature.

Weblinks

For more information, visit
http://www.open.edu/openlearncreate/mod/oucontent/view.php?id=79940&printable=1
Last accessed on 31/July/2020

Across the Boundary 2

A. Interview a few people from your locality who have migrated from other places. They can be people working at your house, neighbours or vegetable vendors from your locality. Find the following information about them:

1. The place to which they belong
2. The factors that compelled them to migrate
3. Why they migrated
4. The number of years they have stayed in the locality
5. The average number of times they visit their native place in a year

B. The graph shows the composition of the immigrants in Norway from 1970 to 2016. Study the graph and answer the questions.

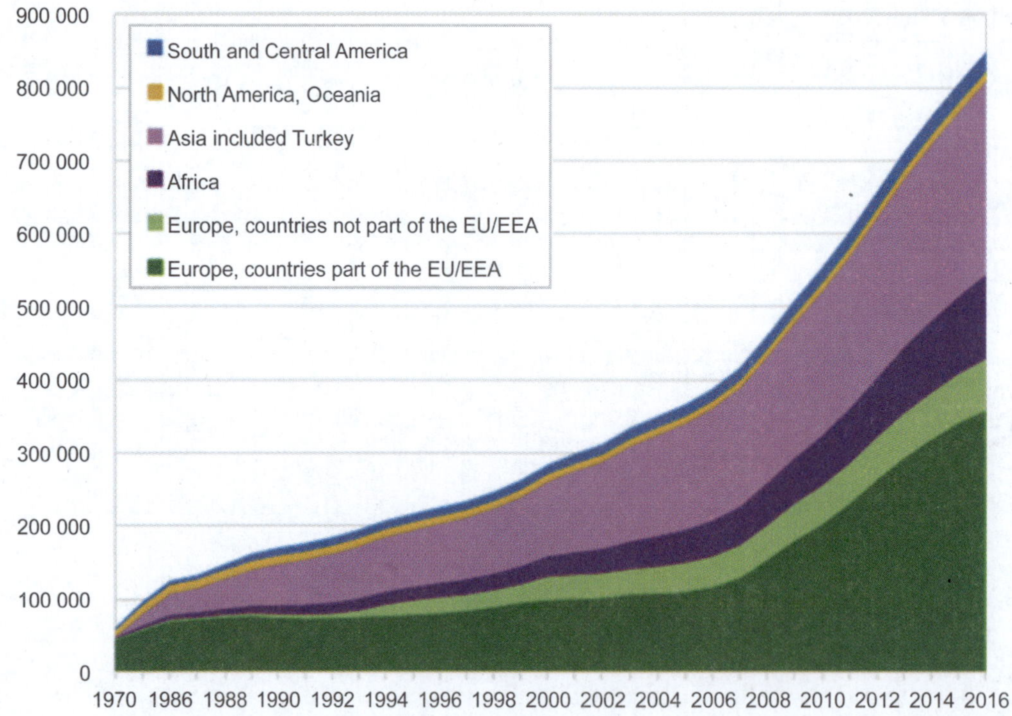

Source: Statistics Norway.

1. People from which nationality have migrated most to Norway?
2. People from which nationality have migrated least to Norway?
3. State the possible reasons why people migrate to Norway.
4. State the reason why Norway supported this migration.
5. Explain the population composition of Norway.

Theme 3

Disaster Management

Disaster management is an essential part of studying geography as it deals with the causes and impacts of natural or man-made disasters and the ways to cope with their aftermath. Disasters are sudden calamities with a potential to cause widespread destruction of infrastructure, devastation of the environment and loss of human life. They affect the economic, social and cultural life of an individual as well as that of the entire society. Disaster management deals with preparing vulnerable communities to cope with the destruction caused by disasters. Simultaneously, it tries to spread awareness about the ways of coping with loss and dealing with emergency situations. In the upcoming chapters, we will learn about natural and man-made hazards and how these hazards affect populations. We will also learn about the safety measures to be taken during these disasters to minimize damage. Case studies will help us analyze some of the worst disasters that occurred in the world and the lessons learnt from them.

6 Disaster Management

Let's learn about...

- definition of a disaster.
- difference between natural and man-made hazards.
- disaster management and disaster management cycle.
- role of the government in responding to disasters.

Key Terms

- disasters
- hazard
- vulnerability
- capacity
- relief
- risk
- disaster management

Reflect

Here are a few snippets from newspapers. What do you think is common among all of these?

- In the year 1923, more than 13 lakh people were killed in a post-earthquake fire in Tokyo.
- In December 1984, the Bhopal Gas Tragedy claimed many lives due to the release of a deadly gas from a chemical factory.
- In April 1986, the Chernobyl disaster took place in a nuclear power plant in Ukraine, which claimed the lives of lakhs of people.
- On 26 May 2001, a major earthquake struck Bhuj in Gujarat. Nearly 20,000 casualties were reported.

Throughout the ages, disasters have disrupted human settlements. A disaster is an undesirable calamity that occurs due to forces outside human control. It strikes suddenly, without any warning.

Defining Disaster

The Disaster Management Act of 2005 defines a disaster as 'a catastrophe, mishap, calamity or grave occurrence in any area, arising from natural or man-made causes, or by accident or negligence which result in substantial loss of life or human suffering or damage to, and destruction of, property, or damage to, or degradation of, environment, and is of such a nature or magnitude as to be beyond the coping capacity of the community of the affected area.'

FactPedia

A pandemic is a disease prevalent over a whole country or the world. Some of the worst pandemics humanity has witnessed are the Black Death, the Great Plague of London and the Spanish Flu. In the 21st century, we have had major outbreaks like SARS, ebola and corona virus (covid 19).

According to the United Nations Office for Disaster Risk Reduction, a disaster is 'a serious disruption of the functioning of a community or society involving widespread human, material, economic or environmental losses and impacts, which exceeds the ability of the affected community or society to cope with using its own resources.'

A disaster is usually a combination of hazard, vulnerability and insufficient capacity to reduce the potential chances of risk. While a hazard is a triggering event, vulnerability includes inadequate access to resources and a lack of awareness about the disaster. Let us learn more about these concepts.

Hazard

A hazard is a dangerous condition or event that has the potential of causing injury to life or damage to property or the environment. Hazards can be natural or man-made. Natural hazards are caused by natural phenomena. Man-made hazards are caused because of human negligence.

Types of natural hazards

- **Meteorological**: These are natural events that are caused by the weather and atmospheric conditions that last a few minutes or days. For example, sandstorms, cyclones and cloudbursts.
- **Geophysical**: These are natural events caused due to the movement of the Earth's crust. Some examples are earthquakes, tsunamis and volcanic eruptions.
- **Climatological**: These are events caused by extreme weather conditions that last a few years. Drought is an example.
- **Hydrological**: These are natural events caused by the overflow of water. Floods and landslides are some examples.

Types of man-made hazards

- **Nuclear and radiological**: These are caused by the release of harmful radiations from a nuclear plant or by malfunction of equipment, sometimes triggered by natural hazards, such as earthquakes.
- **Chemical industrial disaster**: These occur due to mishaps in the chemical industry.
- **Fire:** This is caused by human interference. Disasters caused by fire can occur in both residential and non-residential areas. Fire causes a lot of damage to life and property.

By now, you might have seen two terms are being used quite often—hazard and disaster. Are they the same? The term 'hazard' is very closely associated with disaster. Often people tend to confuse the two terms. Hazards are natural phenomena that have the potential to cause disaster. For example, the northeastern part of India is prone to landslides. During the monsoon, this area becomes vulnerable. Thus, protection from landslides becomes essential or it might cause loss of life and property. Landslides are a natural hazard and the destruction they cause makes them a disaster. The impact of the disaster is analyzed by the extent of socio-economic and environmental losses it causes.

Vulnerability is the extent to which a region, a structure, a community and services are likely to be damaged or disrupted by the impact of a particular hazard.

The resources, means and strength that enable communities and households to cope, withstand, mitigate or quickly recover from a disaster is called **capacity**.

Risk is the measure of expected losses due to a hazard occurring in a particular area at a specific time.

Disaster Management

Disaster management aims to reduce or avoid potential losses from hazards, assure prompt and appropriate assistance to victims of disaster and achieve rapid and effective recovery. Disaster management does not eradicate the threat arising from the hazard but emphasizes creating plans and strategies to reduce the adverse effects of the hazard.

A flooded road in Varanasi, India

Disaster management has two components, namely risk management and crisis management. Disaster management includes all the activities, programmes and measures that can be taken before, during and after a disaster, while risk management aims to avoid a disaster, reduce its impact or recover from its devastating effects.

DIY

Find out if your city or town is prone to any natural disasters. Conduct an informal discussion with your family members about the safety measures to be taken during the disaster. You can make a checklist using a chart paper and keep it in your living room.

Disaster management cycle

A disaster management cycle is a process by which governments and civil societies plan for and reduce the impact of disasters. It involves reacting during and immediately after a disaster and taking steps to recover. Appropriate action at all points in the disaster management cycle leads to better preparedness, better warnings, reduced vulnerability and prevention of disasters. A complete disaster management cycle includes the shaping of public policies and plans that either modify the causes of disasters or mitigate their effects on people, property and infrastructure.

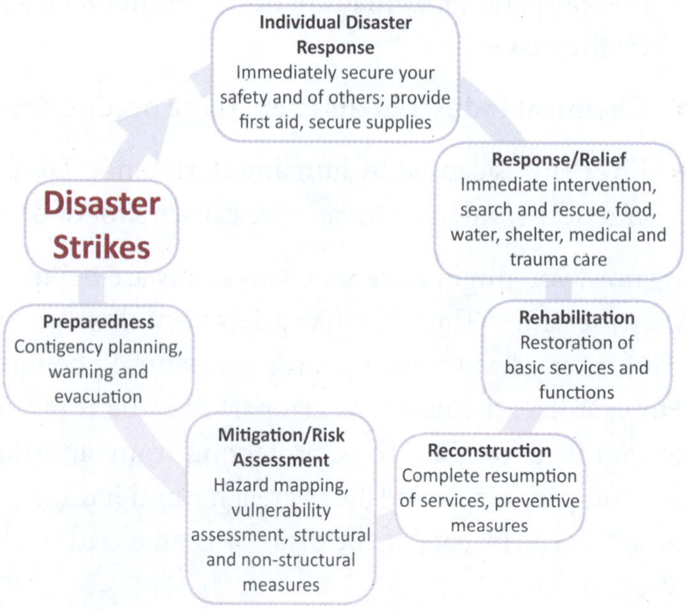

Disaster management cycle

A disaster management cycle has four stages—mitigation, preparedness, response and recovery. However, these steps do not occur in any particular order and often overlap with each other.

Mitigation

Mitigation activities eliminate or reduce the probability of the occurrence of a disaster or reduce the effects of unavoidable disasters. A few mitigation measures are given below.

- Reviewing building materials and building-use regulations
- Vulnerability analysis
- Zoning and land use management
- Planning and implementing preventive health measures
- Creating awareness among the public on simple measures they can adopt to limit loss or injury during a disaster

FactPedia

The Hyogo Framework for Action is a ten-year plan to make the world safe from natural hazards. It provides guiding principles, priorities for action and practical means of achieving disaster resilience in vulnerable communities.

Mitigation is usually carried out with the help of regulations, land use and building practices and steps that reduce or eliminate long-term risk from hazards and their effects. For example, in the aftermath of the 1999 Odisha cyclone, the government decided to construct multipurpose cyclone shelters along the coast to provide safe shelters to vulnerable people.

Preparedness

The goal of preparedness activities is to achieve a satisfactory level of readiness to respond to any emergency situation. Programmes to strengthen the capacity of governments, organizations and communities are a few ways to induce preparedness. A few preparedness measures are:

- response mechanism and procedures
- emergency training and communication systems
- evacuation plans and training
- early warning systems
- creating resource inventories such as reserves of food, equipment, water and medicines
- public information and education

Tsunami warning sign-evacuation route, Kamakura-Japan

During the preparedness phase, governments, organizations and individuals develop plans to save lives, minimize disaster damage and enhance disaster response operations.

vulnerability: the extent to which a region, a structure, a community and services are likely to be damaged or disrupted by the impact of a particular hazard; inventories: a complete list of items such as property, goods in stock, or the contents of a building

Response

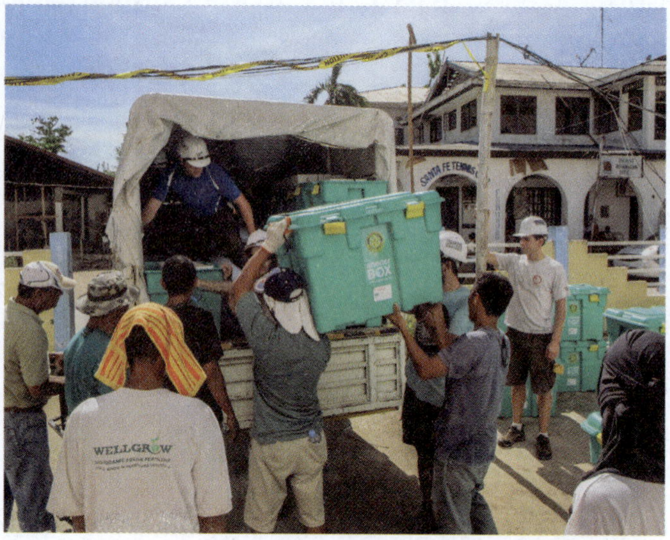

Humanitarian aid workers loading relief material

The aim of emergency response is to provide immediate assistance to maintain life, improve health and support the morale of the affected population. Such assistance may range from providing specific but limited aid, such as assisting refugees with transport, temporary shelter and food, to establishing semi-permanent settlement in camps and other locations. It may also involve initial repairs to damaged infrastructure. The focus in the response phase is on meeting the basic needs of the people until more permanent and sustainable solutions can be found. Humanitarian organizations often participate in this phase of the disaster management cycle.

Recovery

Recovery refers to programmes which go beyond the provision of immediate relief to assist those who have suffered the full impact of a disaster. This may include rebuilding homes or strengthening the capacity to cope with future disasters.

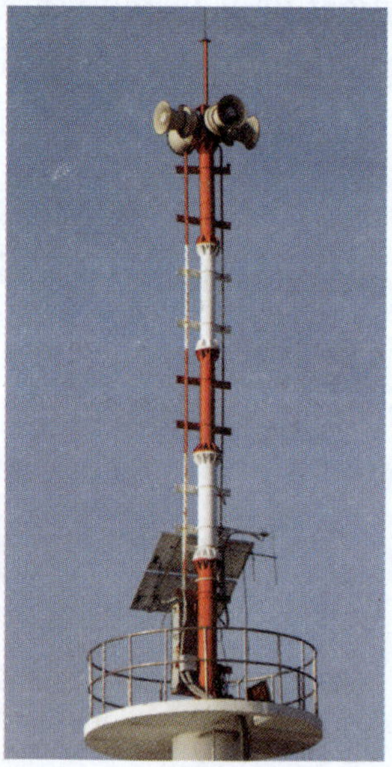

A tsunami warning tower in Thailand

Recovery measures, both short and long term, include:

- returning vital life-support systems to minimum operating standards
- temporary housing
- health and safety education
- reconstruction
- counselling programmes

In case of a disaster, locals are often the first to handle the crisis before external aid can come to the rescue. Thus, they should be well-equipped and know the course of action to be taken. The government, at the national and state level, must also be fully prepared to handle all kinds of disasters. The government has special organs for effective disaster management. The National Disaster Management Plan (NDMP) provides the framework covering all aspects of the disaster management cycle.

Figure Out

Using a map, identify the hazard-prone regions of India. Select any one hazard and mark the states that can be affected by this hazard.

National Organizations for Disaster Management	
Cabinet Committee on Security (CCS)	■ Gives directions necessary for disaster prevention, mitigation, preparedness and effective response
National Crisis Management Committee (NCMC)	■ Gives directions to the crisis management group and suggestions for specific actions to face the crisis
National Disaster Management Authority (NDMA)	■ Makes policies, plans and guidelines for disaster management for central as well as state organizations
National Executive Committee (NEC)	■ Coordinates response in the event of threatening disaster situations or disasters such as flood and earthquake
National Disaster Response Force (NDRF)	■ A group of specially trained force headed by a Director-General, structured like a paramilitary force for rapid placement; carries out rescue operations
National Institute of Disaster Management (NIDM)	■ Carries out human resources development and capacity building for disaster management within the broad policies and guidelines laid down by the NDMA ■ Develops educational materials for training and promoting awareness

Role of State, District and Local Bodies

Disasters occur unexpectedly and cause tremendous loss to humanity. The government of India has set up an organization at the central, state and district level to carry out relief work during disasters. The National Disaster Response Force supervises the action taken by the state and the district disaster management authorities. The disaster management strategies involve rehabilitation and reconstruction plans. It is the primary responsibility of the state and district authorities to monitor and assess the situation and take immediate action as referred to in the guidelines of the National Disaster Management Plan. Apart from these government agencies, the army plays a pivotal role when disaster and emergency strikes. Organizations such as the United Nations and the Red Cross are international organizations that play an important role in responding to disasters.

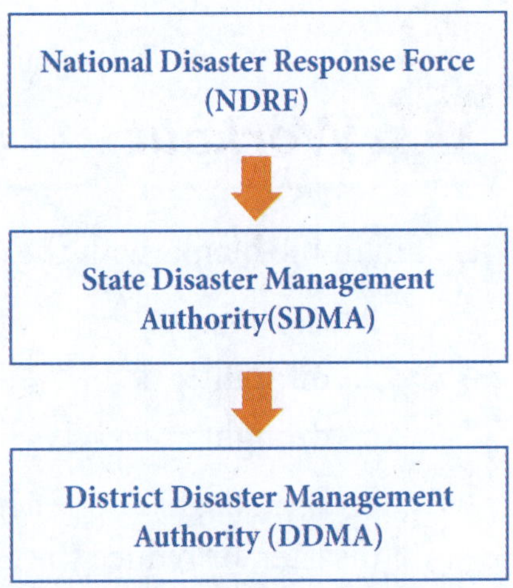

The NDRF directs the state and district authorities to act during disasters

An integrated approach that ensures the involvement of the government, the community and numerous national and international agencies helps and supports people to combat disasters. Prompt and effective response by the authorities minimizes the loss of life, property and environment.

Geo Connect

Thailand is a vulnerable country prone to many natural diasters. It has faced many disasters such as Typhoon Gay in the year 1989, a tsunami in 2004 and a flood in 2011. The Disaster Prevention and Mitigation Act 2007 is the main framework of disaster management in Thailand.

In a Nutshell

- Disasters are incidents that cause significant damage or destruction to life and property or result in a drastic change in the environment.
- A hazard is a dangerous condition or event that has the potential of causing injury to life or damage to property or the environment. Hazards can be natural or man-made.
- Disaster management aims to reduce or avoid potential losses from hazards, assure prompt and appropriate assistance to victims of disaster and achieve rapid and effective recovery.
- A disaster management cycle is a process by which governments and civil societies plan for and reduce the impact of disasters.
- A disaster management cycle has four stages—mitigation, preparedness, response and recovery.
- When disaster strikes, people, government and social organizations should work together to mitigate its impact.

Workout

A. Fill in the blanks with the correct answers.

1. An .... is a man-made hazard.
   - a. oil spill
   - b. earthquake
   - c. drought
   - d. forest fire
2. .... activities eliminate or reduce the probability of the occurrence of a disaster, or reduce the effects of unavoidable disasters.
   - a. Mitigation
   - b. Preparedness
   - c. Response
   - d. Recovery
3. A .... disaster is a man-made disaster.
   - a. geophysical
   - b. hydrological
   - c. climatological
   - d. chemical industrial

B. Write T for true and F for false.

1. The impact of a disaster is analyzed by the extent of socio-economic and environmental losses. ☐
2. An earthquake is a sudden natural hazard. ☐
3. Fire is a natural hazard. ☐
4. The army plays a pivotal role in disaster management. ☐

C. Answer these questions in brief.

1. Define the term 'disaster'.
2. What is the main aim of disaster management?
3. What is mitigation and how is it carried out?
4. Name the four main phases of disaster management.

D. Answer these questions in detail.

1. Explain the main stages of a disaster management cycle.
2. Differentiate between a hazard and a disaster.
3. Explain vulnerability and capacity.
4. What is the role of governmental agencies in disaster management?
5. Name three international organizations involved in disaster management.

Think Box

Which man-made nuclear disaster took place during the Second World War? What were its consequences?

Picture Study

Look at the picture and answer these questions.

1. During which disaster are these vehicles used?
2. How will you contact an official at a fire station in your neighborhood?

Life Skills and Values

Make a diary entry of your hours during lockdown. You can cover the following points:

- Productivity
- Helping out at home
- Taking care of yourself
- Steps you take to follow safety protocol.

Enjoy

Make a rough sketch of a disaster control room. The control room should have:

a. an emergency communication system that includes devices such as satellite phones, GPS devices, laptops and mobile phones.

b. rescue kits that include emergency items such as flash lights, food supplies, blankets and medicine.

Present your sketch in the classroom.

Weblinks

For more information, visit
https://www.nationalgeographic.com/environment/natural-disasters-weather/
Last accessed on 31/July/2020

7 Safety and Disasters

Let's learn about...

- causes and impacts of an earthquake.
- causes and impacts of floods.
- causes and impacts of fires.
- safety measures taken during earthquakes, floods and fires.

Key Terms

- hazard
- disaster
- earthquake
- flood
- fire
- safety

Reflect

Read the passage and answer the questions.

Kanchan stays in a small village on the banks of the river Damodar in West Bengal. Her village is flooded almost every year during the monsoon. The District Disaster Management Team has assembled and trained a small group in the village that carries out mock drills each month so as to know how to stay safe during the floods. An NGO along with the villagers has built a shelter house on a small hillock near the outskirts of the village. The villagers take shelter in it during the floods. Mock drills are practised in the shelter house once a month. However, just before the rainy season, it is practised once a week. Kanchan and her friends have joined the volunteer team. Last month, they performed a street play to create awareness about flood safety. One morning, there was a flood alert. Kanchan along with her villagers moved into the shelter house with basic necessities.

1. Is flood a disaster associated with the weather or geography of a place?
2. Why do you think the district authority has developed a disaster management team comprising the locals?
3. Which mitigation method have the villagers adopted?

In the previous chapter, we read about different disaster management strategies. We also learnt that the main aim of disaster management is to reduce the effect of the hazard and the loss to life, property and environment. Let us learn about the mitigation methods that can be employed during natural disasters.

mitigation: the action of reducing the severity, seriousness or painfulness of something

Earthquake

Destruction caused by an earthquake

An earthquake is a natural phenomenon that occurs abruptly. Earthquakes cause sudden shaking or trembling of the Earth's surface due to internal pressure within the Earth's crust. Earthquakes are amongst the most terrifying of all natural phenomena as they cause a huge loss of life and property.

Causes of earthquakes

The surface of the Earth is made up of seven large lithospheric plates. The place where these lithospheric plates meet are called fractures or faults. A fault is a facture in the Earth's crust. They are zones of weakness, and the movement of the lithospheric plates occurs along these faults. The main cause of earthquakes is the sudden slipping of the lithospheric plates along the faults. Earthquakes can also occur because of volcanic eruptions. The shaking caused by earthquakes is called seismic waves. Seismologists study seismic waves and measure the intensity of the earthquakes. The point at which an earthquake originates is called the seismic focus. The point on the Earth's surface directly above the seismic focus is called an epicentre. An earthquake causes the most destruction at the epicentre.

The United Nations workers providing relief

The magnitude of an earthquake is greater if its seismic focus is near the Earth's surface. The magnitude of an earthquake is measured with a Richter scale.

The largest number of earthquakes occur in the following zones of the Earth:

- Zone One: It extends around the Pacific Ocean, which includes the western coasts of the Americas, Central America and the West Indies.
- Zone Two: It is located in the Indonesian archipelago and the Himalayan region. It stretches further to the Hindu Kush Range, some regions of the Caucasus and the Atlas Mountains.
- Zone Three: It comprises Japan, Chile, Italy, the Philippines and California.

Impact of earthquakes

Earthquakes cause changes to the Earth's surface. People can neither predict an earthquake nor prevent it. However, seismologists can map earthquake-prone regions of the world. In these regions, special mitigation methods are adopted to reduce the impact of an earthquake.

Some impacts of an earthquake are given below.

- Landslides
- Large-scale destruction as buildings collapse
- Serious fires
- Roads and railways cave in
- Tsunamis if the earthquake originates below the sea or on the sea floor, causing unprecedented damage to life and infrastructure

People carrying food provided by relief teams

DIY

On 29 September 1993, an earthquake of magnitude 6.4 hit Latur in Maharashtra. According to researchers, the factors that had contributed to the devastating disaster were:

- High population density in the affected region
- Poor construction of buildings

Discuss how faulty construction increases the destruction caused by an earthquake.

Preparedness and preventive measures for earthquakes		
Before	**During**	**After**
Study the seismic map and find out which seismic zone your area is located in.	Stay calm.	Check for injuries.
Make an evacuation plan as suggested by the disaster management team of your locality.	If indoors: • Stand against a wall near the centre of the building. • Stand in the doorway. • Stay away from windows. • Stay away from glass furniture and wall hangings. • Crawl underneath wooden furniture.	Do not enter any partially damaged areas. Expect aftershocks.

unprecedented: exceptionally

Choose a safe place in your room in case you are unable to evacuate. The safe places can be beneath wooden furniture.	If outdoors: • stay away from power lines, lamp posts and telephone lines. • find a clear spot away from buildings. • avoid bridges and flyovers that might be damaged during the earthquake.	Watch out for power lines, broken gas pipes and cracks on the roads.
Choose a safe place, stay away from glass windows and glass furniture	If in a car: • slow down and find a safe place. • stay in the car until the tremors stop.	To eliminate fire hazard, check the gas cylinder.

Floods

Floods are natural disasters. They occur when incessant and heavy rainfall causes water bodies to swell. Excess water overflows and fills in the nearby areas. Buildings, farms and roads are submerged causing destruction. Floods can also occur due to cloudbursts. Such floods are called flash floods. Flash floods occur within 2 to 6 hours and sometimes within a few seconds. Slow floods occur slowly and can last for days and weeks. They usually spread over many kilometres.

Floods disrupt the normal lives of people

Let us learn about the causes of floods and how they impact human life and environment.

Causes of floods

Some of the causes of floods are:

Figure Out
Name three flood-prone regions of India.

- Heavy rains are the most common causes of floods. Floods are common during the monsoon. Heavy rainfall fills lakes and rivers beyond their holding capacity. As a result, they breach their banks, and water inundates the adjoining areas. For example, Mumbai and Chennai often face the threat of floods during monsoon.
- The coastal regions experience frequent and powerful cyclones. The sea water carried by powerful winds enters coastal regions and floods them.
- Dams are built on rivers to harness river water for generating hydroelectricity and for irrigation. Sometimes, when the volume of water in the dam increases beyond capacity, the dam can break and submerge surrounding areas. Thus, excess water is released from the dam to prevent it from breaking, which results in flooding of the catchment area.

incessant: continuous; inundate: submerge

Impact of floods

The impact of floods are given below.

- Flood water submerges fields and destroys crops causing much loss to farmers.
- Floods damage houses and property making people homeless.
- Fast-moving floodwater carries away the fertile top soil, washing off important nutrients present in the soil.
- Floods harm livestock.
- Floods are often followed by epidemics such as cholera. This adversely affects the health of humans, animals and even plants.

Floods can make people homeless

Preparedness and preventive measures for floods		
Before	**During**	**After**
Check the flood zones of India. Find out the zone in which your area is located.	As soon as flood warning is signaled, we should try to move to a safer area.	Try to contact the disaster management team.
Find the nearest relief centre. Find out the safest and easiest route to relief camps.	Turn off all the electrical appliances, gas stoves and heating appliances before evacuating.	Do not rush back to your houses without a rescue team member's help.
Memorize all emergency numbers and important phone numbers. Follow weather reports on television or radio.	Leave the flooded area as soon as possible. Carry a walking stick as the water will have a high undercurrent.	Enter your house only when water has receded. Turn off all electrical appliances till then.
Keep an emergency kit ready. This kit should include first aid box, dry food, flashlight and waterproof clothes.	Stay away from power lines or broken power transmission cables to avoid accidents.	Thoroughly clean all the items in your house before you use them again. Discard items that may have decomposed in water.
Make sure you store medicines that will help combat common illnesses like colds, fever and diarrohea along with other medicines, which you or other family members need to take.	Try to keep away from flood water as it may contain other hazardous materials.	Wear masks and gloves before cleaning the house and surroundings.

Keep all necessary documents, medicines and valuables on a high shelf or a cupboard.	Keep yourself updated about the weather report.	Keep antiseptic ointment and medicines as recommended by the disaster management team.
Plants reduce the flow of water. Therefore, plant a lot of trees in your compound and locality to control the flow and speed of water.	Put chlorine tablets to purify the drinking water as waterborne diseases are very common during floods.	Drink clean water and wash leafy vegetables with lukewarm water.

Fire

Fire is a combination of heat and light. It is a major cause of destruction. Let us read about some fires that cause damage to life and property.

Figure Out

Is fire extinguished quickly with hot water or cold water?

Causes of fire

Industrial fires and explosions cause loss of life and damage to property. Industrial fires mainly occur because of the following reasons.

- Combustible dust is a major cause of fire in food processing industries, chemical industries and manufacturing industries.
- Fire is also caused by the sparks generated from heavy machinery.
- Flammable substances used in the chemical industry lead to fires.
- Faulty wiring used in the industries cause fire.

An industrial fire

Fire in residential areas can occur in urban or a rural localities due to the following reasons:

- Overpopulation and massive migration has led to an abrupt increase in the urban population. Fire spreads rapidly in high population density regions.
- Many houses are not constructed according to building codes. Poor electrical wiring and faulty electrical appliances are major causes of fire. Kitchen fires are often caused by cooking methods such as frying, boiling and simmering.
- Fire in a market place is also common. Unplanned and cluttered shops make the place susceptible to fire. Storing flammable substances is a major source of fire.
- Houses in rural areas that have thatched roofs are vulnerable to fires.

Fire in a residential area

Lightning is the most common cause of natural **forest fires.** It mostly occurs during dry lightning with little or no rain. Some forest fires occur because of overheating of the biomass due to natural causes. However, most of the forest fires occur because of human negligence. These accidental fires are caused by campers, hikers or others traveling through forests or by garbage burners.

Preparedness and preventive measures for fires		
Before	**During**	**After**
Smoke and carbon monoxide detectors and fire alarms must be installed in buildings.	If your clothes catch fire, you should remember to stop, drop and roll until the fire is extinguished.	Do not enter the building again unless the fire has been completely put out and the building is safe.
Use safe cooking appliances in the kitchen. Cotton towels, pot holders and curtains should be kept away from the stove.	Go to the nearest telephone or find a mobile phone and call the fire station.	If you are a burn victim or want to save a burn victim call the emergency number at the nearest hospital.
Make an escape plan with proper routes. Find out where the fire exits are located in buildings you frequent.	Be sure that you take the safest way to escape from the house. Ensure that fire or smoke is not blocking your way.	Wait for further instruction before entering the building again.
Store flammable substances away from sources of fire.	Do not hide anywhere inside the building. Run out of the building and move to a safe open place.	Inspect the electric wiring regularly, and check the extension cords and outlets.
Practise fire mock drills.	To escape during a fire, fall and crawl. It is easier to breathe in a fire if you stay low while getting out. Use the back of your hand to test if a door is hot before you open it. If it is hot, try to use another way out.	Keep a first-aid box ready for minor burns.

Geo Connect

The Federal Emergency Management Agency (FEMA), was created in June 1978 with the purpose of responding to disasters in the USA. The agency has its headquarters in Washington D.C.

In a Nutshell

- Earthquakes are natural phenomena and occur suddenly. They cause many changes to the Earth's surface.
- Floods are caused by natural and man-made reasons. They impact the socio-economic lives of people.
- Fires are disasters that can occur because of both natural and man-made causes.

Workout

A. Fill in the blanks with the correct answers.

1. The tremors caused by earthquakes are called ....
   a. seismic waves b. volcanic activity c. fault lines d. crests
2. Japan, Chile and Italy belong to .... earthquake zone.
   a. zone two b. zone one c. zone three d. zone four
3. .... occur within 2 to 6 hours and sometimes within seconds.
   a. Droughts b. Flashfloods c. Earthquakes d. Fires
4. Electrical hazards cause ....
   a. floods b. fires c. earthquakes d. tsunami
5. Earthquakes occur along the .... of the Earth's crust.
   a. oceanic plates b. fault lines c. seismic lines d. earthquake lines

B. Answer these questions in brief.

1. Name the major earthquake zones of the Earth.
2. What are seismic waves?
3. Name two types of mitigation strategies for earthquakes.
4. Describe the types of floods.
5. What is an industrial fire?

C. Answer these questions in detail.

1. What are the effects of an earthquake?
2. Write five safety measures one should take during an earthquake.
3. What are the major causes of flood?
4. Explain the safety measures one should take during floods.
5. What are the major causes of fires?

Think Box

Find out what is carbon monoxide poisoning and how one can stay safe from it.

Picture Study

Look at the picture and answer these questions.

1. Who are the officers wearing the uniforms?
2. How do they help us during earthquakes?

Life Skills and Values

There are three types of burns:

First degree burns: These are mild burns. They mainly affect the outer layer of the skin.

Second degree burns: These burns affect the inner layers of skin. They cause pain, redness, swelling and blistering.

Third degree burns: These are the most serious type of burns. They affect the deeper tissues of the skin.

Invite a doctor to your school. Arrange a small discussion with the doctor asking him or her explain the type of burns and the first-aid required to treat them. Prepare a report based on the discussion and publish it in your school magazine.

Enjoy

Make a first-aid box. You will need items such as band aids, gauze bandages, white cloth tape, a pair of scissors, an antiseptic ointment and a burn cream.

Weblinks

For more information, visit
http://www.ndma.gov.in/en/media-public-awareness/kids-section/school-safety.html
Last accessed on 31/July/2020

8 Assam Floods

Let's learn about...

- 2016 Assam floods.
- reasons for floods in Assam.
- destruction caused during the Assam floods.
- relief work during the Assam floods.

Key Terms

- floods
- destruction
- one-horned rhinoceros
- Assam
- Kaziranga

Reflect

Hundreds of school children are affected almost every year by natural or man-made disasters. Find out if your school is disaster-ready. Examine your school building and make a note of the things that might be dangerous to students in the event of a disaster.

In 2016, Assam experienced unusually heavy monsoon rains; consequently, many parts of the state were flooded. Flooding is seasonal in Assam on account of the monsoon, which lasts from June to September. The flood is believed to have affected nearly 1.8 million people. The Kaziranga National Park was almost completely submerged during this flood causing an unprecedented loss to the wildlife of the state. The Pobitora Wildlife Sanctuary was also affected during the flood.

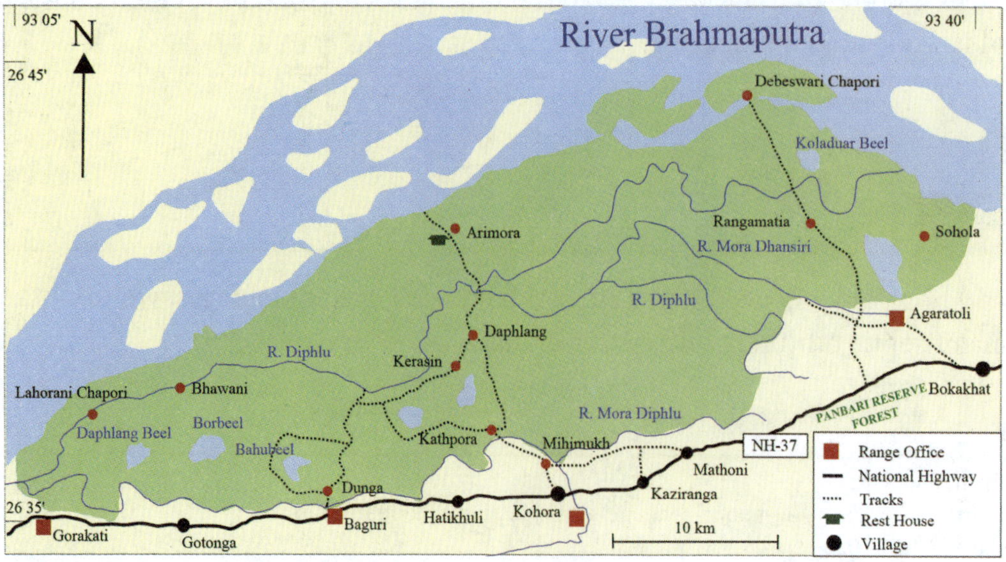

Flood prone region of Assam

Location

Assam is located in the northeastern region of India. The river Brahmaputra flows through Assam and influences its socio-economic life. It is the sixth largest river in the world in terms of the volume of water it carries. It has 41 tributaries, out of which, 26 join the river on its northern bank and the rest join the river on its southern bank.

Districts affected: 22

Number of people affected: 17.94 lakh

Total cultivated area affected: 2, 13, 251 hectares

Worse hit districts: Morigaon, Jorhat, Dhubri, Barpeta, Lakhimpur, Golaghat, Sonitpur, Goalpara, Bongaigaon, Dhemaji and Darrang

Number of relief camps: 517

Relief distribution centres: 186; they sheltered about 2,29,554 people

Causes of the Floods

The river Brahmaputra gets flooded because of the following reasons:

- The Brahmaputra Valley along with the northeastern hills receive heavy monsoon showers. The average rainfall of this region exceeds 2480 mm annually.
- The snowmelt originating from the source of the Brahmaputra, near Manasarovar, also increases its water level.
- Assam is a valley located in the south of the Eastern Himalayas. The land is mostly composed of soft rocks, which easily give a way to gushing water of the flood.
- Assam lies in an seismically active zone, that is, it is prone to earthquakes. Geologists believe that the river Brahmaputra has become unstable after the region experienced earthquakes. The earthquake of 1950 made massive changes in the topography of the Brahmaputra Valley.
- Assam is densely populated along the banks of Brahmaputra and its tributaries. The rapid growth of settlements and construction of railway bridges on the river and its tributaries has disrupted the natural flow and speed of the river. Therefore, the river water breaches embankments and flows out to vulnerable areas causing floods. The lack of a proper drainage system also increases the flow of water on the ground. Deforestation in the Brahmaputra Valley has resulted in increased siltation, decreasing the depth of the river basin.

Figure Out

Why is the river Damodar known as the 'sorrow of Bengal'?

Majuli in Assam was affected badly during the floods

siltation: a process by which water becomes dirty because of the fine mineral particles in the it

Impact on Human Life

- Over 1,100,600 people were affected by the floods in Assam. The people living on sand islands of the Brahmaputra river were completely marooned.
- Roads were submerged and many were closed across the state. In rural areas, roads were blocked by debris left behind by landslides and erosion.
- Tremendous damage was caused to the infrastructure, including bridges and communication networks.
- Majuli, an island in Jorhat, was completely cut off from the rest of the state. Thousands of people were stranded on this island without access to essential services.
- Many people who could not reach the relief camps went missing, and many people were displaced and forced to migrate to safer regions.

Flood in Kothari village, Assam

Kaziranga National Park

Impact on Wildlife

Almost 80 per cent of the land area in Kaziranga National Park was submerged in flood water. Around 300 wild animals drowned. This included 21 Indian one-horned rhinoceroses and about 219 Indian hog deers.

Rescue and Relief

Most of the rescue and relief work during the 2016 Assam floods was conducted by the National Disaster Response Force and the Assam State Disaster Management Authority (ASDMA). The army was mobilized to monitor the flood situation and coordinate relief efforts. Helicopters and boats were used to evacuate people. Around 500 temporary relief centres and 50 distribution centres were set up by the state government. Food, medicine and clothes were provided in relief camps.

FactPedia

Chang ghor or silt houses are houses made on pillars of bamboo. This is done to allow the water to flow underneath the houses without causing any damage to the building during floods. The pillars are made of bamboo, which is water resistant.

marooned: being trapped on an island

DIY

Prepare a short report on the 2014 India-Pakistan Floods.

You can focus on the following.

1. Origin of the disaster
2. Affected regions
3. Consequences
4. Rescue and relief operations

Government Initiatives

The Assam Disaster Management Authority (ASDMA) is widening its scope to reduce the impact of floods. Assam floods are a repetitive disaster and an integrated flood management system is required. Some of the steps that can be taken to avoid floods or reduce the impacts of floods are as follows:

- The institutional roles and responsibilities of different administration offices, like the office of the district magistrate, block development office and village panchayat in disaster management should be clearly defined.
- Water, sanitation and health are major issues in the aftermath of cyclones and floods and a speedy response are crucial to prevent the spread of diseases.
- The National Disaster Management Authority (NDMA) should seek the help of international organizations like UNDP, WHO and UNICEF, which was absent during the Assam floods.
- Implementing an improved flood control warning system can reduce the damage caused by floods. Improved forecasting, early warning system and preparedness measures should be adopted to reduce the number of lives lost and impact on livelihoods.

Geo Connect

The Yellow River, also known as Huang Ho, is China's second-longest river. The 1931 flooding of this river is considered the deadliest natural disaster in history. China has tried to control the flooding of this river by building overflow channels and dykes.

In a Nutshell

- Assam is located in the northeastern region of the country, which receives rainfall from the southwest monsoon winds lasting for four months.
- The river Brahmaputra flows through the entire state and thus influences the socio-economic life of Assam. It has 41 tributaries.
- The river Brahmaputra gets flooded because of heavy monsoon showers, snowmelt from the source of the river, soft rocks in the region which give way to gushing of flood water, it lies in a seismic zone and it is densely populated.
- Over 1,100,600 people were affected by floods in Assam and almost 80 per cent of the land in Kaziranga National Park was submerged killing over 300 wild animals.
- Most of the rescue and relief work during the 2016 Assam floods was conducted by the National Disaster Response Force and the Assam State Disaster Management Authority (ASDMA).

Workout

A. Fill in the blanks with the correct answers.

1. The Kaziranga National Park and .... were affected by the 2016 Assam floods.
   a. Pobitora Wildlife Sanctuary b. Manas Wildlife Sanctuary
   c. Gir Natinal Park d. Ranthambore National Park
2. Assam receives monsoon rains from ....
   a. January to September b. March to September
   c. December to March d. June to September
3. Assam is located in the .... Himalayas.
   a. eastern b. western c. northeastern d. northwestern
4. The river Brahmaputra has .... tributaries.
   a. 20 b. 15 c. 41 d. 26
5. A total of .... districts were affected by the Assam floods.
   a. 12 b. 13 c. 22 d. 25

B. Answer these questions in detail.

1. Explain the reasons that lead to the Assam floods of 2016.
2. What were the impacts of the Assam floods?
3. Why is the river Brahmaputra prone to flooding?
4. Explain the relief and rescue work carried out by the government during the 2016 Assam floods.

Think Box

How did the 2016 Assam floods affect the health of the people of this region. Name the diseases that were spread by the flood water.

Picture Study

Look at the picture and answer these questions.

1. Why is the Indian one-horned rhinoceros endangered?
2. How were they affected during the 2016 Assam floods?

Life Skills and Values

How do you think members of a community can help each other during natural disasters. What do you think your responsibilities are as a community member and how would you help others during a natural disaster?

Enjoy

On a map of India, mark the regions where the following endangered animals are found:

1. Ganges River Dolphin
2. Red Panda
3. Royal Bengal Tiger
4. Show Leopard

Make chart and find out the estimated population, habitat and distribution and conservation challenges for each animal. Present the chart in the classroom.

Weblinks

For more information, visit
https://www.wti.org.in/tag/assam-floods/
Last accessed on 31/July/2020

9 Nepal Earthquake

Let's learn about...

- causes of the 2015 Nepal earthquake.
- impacts of the 2015 Nepal earthquake.
- rescue and relief during the 2015 Nepal earthquake.

Key Terms

- Nepal
- earthquake
- natural disasters
- relief
- rescue

Reflect

Read the passage and answer the questions.

The Red Cross appealed for a funding of U.S. $93m to help 7,00,000 vulnerable people for two years from the recent earthquake in Nepal. The group was closely coordinating with the government and humanitarian agencies to provide relief to those who needed it.

1. What is the Red Cross?
2. How and when does it help the people?

Nepal is a landlocked country located in the central Himalayan region. It is one of the most seismically active regions of the world. The Himalayas are young fold mountains that were formed due to the collision of the Indo-European plate and the Eurasian plate. The Himalayas are gradually rising in height, which explains the proneness of this region to earthquakes.

Nepal experienced a powerful earthquake of magnitude 7.8 on the morning of 25 April, 2015. Its epicentre was located 74 kilometres northwest of Kathmandu, near the Lamjung district of Nepal. Within an hour of the initial shock, two more aftershocks of magnitudes 6.6 and 6.7 jolted the region. On May 12, an aftershock of magnitude 7.3, struck Nepal's Dolakha district, approximately

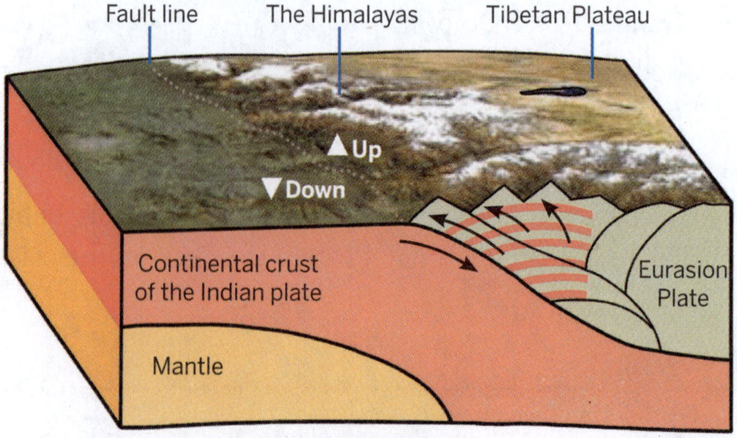

Continental Collision

76 kilometres northeast of Kathmandu. The tremors were felt in northern India, northwestern Bangladesh and in parts of Tibet and Bhutan. The earthquake also triggered a massive avalanche on Mount Everest.

Main cities of Nepal

Causes of the Earthquake

The earthquake was caused by thrust faulting along the major fault line of the Earth's crust located in the Indus-Yarlung suture zone. The Eurasian plate is slowly slipping under the Indian plate along this fault line. This tectonic activity is responsible for the increase in the height of the Himalayas every year. The effects of this earthquake were amplified because Kathmandu basin is made of soft sedimentary rocks that collapse easily.

FactPedia

The 1934 Bihar-Nepal earthquake had a magnitude of 8.0 and is considered as one of the worst earthquakes that hit Nepal.

Figure Out

Find out the names of the heritage sites of Nepal that were damaged by the earthquake.

Impacts of the Earthquake

- The number of casualties was reported to be around 8,800. More than 20,000 people suffered serious injuries.
- According to the Nepal Earthquake Assessment Unit, almost 80,000 people were displaced during the earthquake. The most number of displaced people were reported from Dhading, Dolakha, Gorkha, Kathmandu and Sindhupalchowk districts.
- The earthquake caused massive infrastructural damage to Nepal. Thousands of houses were destroyed and many villages and heritage buildings were completely flattened, especially those around the epicentre. This included parts of Taleju Temple and the Dharahara Tower, which collapsed entirely.
- The earthquake triggered avalanches and landslides in the region. The worse-hit region was the Langtang Valley where a three-kilometre-wide avalanche wiped out the entire village of Ghodatabela and Langtang. Nearly 300 people were reported missing from this village.

Destruction caused in Bhaktapur, Kathmandu

- The earthquake triggered an avalanche on Mount Everest that killed 13 mountaineers. Landslides struck a number of villages near Pokhara and destroyed nearly half of the houses in the Lumle village.
- Essential services such as healthcare were suspended or were unaccessible to the people. The Tribhuvan International Airport was closed down and transportation services were temporarily suspended.

Boudha camp in Kathmandu, one of many camps that was set up after the earthquake in Nepal, 2015

- The earthquake adversely affected the economy of Nepal. The total rebuilding cost of the infrastructural damage was around 6 to 8 billion dollars. The tourism sector that provides employment to thousands of people in Nepal suffered a huge setback as tourist destinations were inaccessible. The banking sector also incurred a huge loss.
- In the aftermath of the earthquake, a disease called scrub typhus broke out, which claimed hundreds of lives.
- The earthquake also had a lot of social impacts. People living in the temporary shelters became vulnerable to crime.

DIY

Prepare a short report on the 2005 Kashmir Earthquake.

You can include the following information:

1. Origin of the earthquake
2. Damage caused by the earthquake
3. Aftershocks
4. Relief and rescue work

Rescue and Relief

The rescue operations were carried out by the Nepalese army under Operation Sankat Mochan. It was carried out with the support of the Red Cross. The Indian Army and the United States Marine Corps also carried out relief and rescue operations. The earthquake victims also received relief from many international organizations such as Heifer International, Mercy Corps, World Health Organization and BBC Media Action.

Rescue and relief

Reconstruction

The United Nations Educational, Scientific and Cultural Organization (UNESCO) and the Ministry of Culture of Nepal worked together to build and strengthen the damaged monuments.

Relief, Rehabilitation and Reconstruction Measures

- The government of Nepal constructed temporary safe shelters in 16 different parts of Nepal.
- The government was committed to ensure that all the affected population in the earthquake-hit districts get basic aid and necessary arrangements for resettling.
- The government has made a plan to ensure the building of earthquake resistant structures with local materials and in a cost effective manner.
- The government announced it will rebuild all damaged structures of individuals along with public infrastructure and heritage buildings which were devastated by the earthquake.
- The government made necessary arrangements for providing affected farmers with free of cost seeds and subsidies for fertilizers.

Geo Connect

Indonesia is prone to natural disasters such as earthquakes and tsunamis. Tsunamis are caused by underwater earthquakes. In the year 2004, Indonesia was hit by a tsunami. The earthquake had a magnitude of 9.15 and was one of the worst tsunamis in the world.

In a Nutshell

- Nepal experienced a powerful earthquake of magnitude 7.8 on the morning of 25 April, 2015.
- On May 12, an aftershock of magnitude 7.3, struck Nepal's Dolakha district, approximately 76 kilometres northeast of Kathmandu.
- The earthquake was caused by thrust faulting along the major fault line of the Earth's crust located in the Indus-Yarlung suture zone. The Eurasian Plate is slowly slipping under the Indian Plate along this fault line.
- The number of casualties was reported to be around 8,800. More than 20,000 people suffered serious injuries. Almost 80,000 people were displaced and thousands of houses and heritage buildings were destroyed.
- The earthquake triggered avalanches and landslides in the region as well as an avalanche in Mount Everest killing 13 people.
- The rescue operations were carried out by the Nepalese with the support of the Red Cross. The Indian Army, the United States Marine Corps and international organizations like the Heifer International, Mercy corps, the WHO and BBC Media Action carried out relief and rescue operations.

Workout

A. Fill in the blanks with the correct answers.

1. The epicentre of the 2015 Nepal earthquake was located in the .... district of Nepal.
   a. Lamjung b. Kaski c. Gorkha d. Dolakha
2. The earthquake triggered an avalanche in the ....
   a. Barun Valley b. Langtang Valley c. Khumbu Valley d. Rolwaling Valley
3. The .... suture zone lies in the southern border of Nepal.
   a. Indus-Yarlung b. Indus-Ganga c. Yarlung-Brahmaputra d. Yarlung-Ganga
4. The Nepal earthquake was caused by .... faulting.
   a. thrust b. divergent c. strip stike d. reverse

B. Answer these questions in detail.

1. Explain the causes of the Nepal earthquake.
2. Why is Nepal an earthquake prone region?
3. Explain the impacts of the Nepal earthquake.
4. Explain the relief and recuse work carried out during the Nepal earthquake.

Think Box

Collect information about the plan and building materials used in constructing houses in Japan. Discuss why these buildings are made that way.

Picture Study

Look at the picture and answer these questions.

1. Identify the structure that was damaged during the Nepal earthquake.
2. Name the relief and rescue organizations that helped the people after the Nepal earthquake.

Life Skills and Values

Enact the do's and dont's of an earthquake. Invite your junior classes to observe the different precautionary measures that should be taken during an earthquake.

Enjoy

Make a report on the earthquakes that occurred recently in India and our neighboring countries.

Weblinks

For more information, visit
https://www.mercycorps.org/articles/nepal/quick-facts-what-you-need-know-about-nepal-earthquake
Last accessed on 31/July/2020

10 Deepwater Horizon Oil Spill

Let's learn about...

- the causes of the Deepwater Horizon Oil Spill.
- the impact of the Deepwater Horizon Oil Spill.
- disaster management during the Deepwater Horizon Oil Spill.

Key Terms

- oil spill
- Gulf of Mexico
- controlled burning
- bio remediation

Reflect

Discuss these issues with your classmates.

1. Effects of pollution on marine ecosystem
2. Damage caused because of the marine pollution
3. Cleaning methods employed for oceans and seas

An **oil spill** is the release of liquid petroleum into the environment, especially in marine areas. It is a human-made disaster. It involves the accidental release of oil into a water body. The source of the oil can be a tanker, an offshore drilling rig or an underwater pipeline. It is hazardous to marine life and the environment.

Oil spill on a beach

Location

The Deepwater Horizon oil rig was located in the Gulf of Mexico near the Mississippi river delta in the United States. The rig was installed at Macondo Prospect, an oil-producing region in the Gulf of Mexico. It was owned by an offshore oil-drilling company called Transocean. The rig was leased to the company by British Petroleum (BP). Therefore, the disaster is also referred to as **BP oil spill**. The rig was built in South Korea by Hyundai Heavy Industries.

FactPedia

The British Petroleum is the largest global oil and gas company. It operates in over 80 countries.

The Disaster

Deepwater Horizon rig at a drilling location offshore Louisiana in the Gulf of Mexico

On 20 April 2010, an explosion on the Deepwater Horizon Macondo oil well drilling platform killed 11 workers and started the largest marine oil spill in world history, releasing millions of barrels of oil into the Gulf of Mexico. The Deepwater Horizon Oil Spill was one of the worst oil spills in the history of the world. It is also known as the Gulf of Mexico oil spill.

Causes

According to experts, eight disastrous failures led to the explosion that destroyed the oil rig. This incident occurred because of several technological failures rather than a single one.

Construction material

The borehole at the bottom of the rig was capped with cement to prevent any leakage. The gas and oil began to leak through it into the pipe flowing to the surface.

Eyewitness Account

"We have seen eyeless crabs, soft-shelled crabs and even crabs with shells that did not have their usual spike."

Valve

A valve is a device attached to a pipe or tube that controls the flow of air or a liquid. This device stops, starts or controls the flow of fluid. The pipe that is used to extract oil contains two such mechanical valves. A fault in the valve led to the leakage of methane gas to the surface of the oil rig.

Misinterpretation of pressure data

The staff on duty on the oil rig had carried out various pressure tests to find out whether the valve was operating properly. However, they failed to detect the fault in the valve. They had incorrectly analyzed that the well was properly sealed.

Delayed response

The crew at the surface failed to notice the flow of oil and gas towards the surface. The oil leak was discovered only two days after it actually started.

FactPedia

Blowout preventers are a large, specialized valves or similar mechanical devices, used to seal, control and monitor oil and gas wells to prevent blow out.

Gas alarm

The on-board gas detection system that was supposed to trigger warning failed to work.

Battery failure of the blowout preventer

The explosion destroyed control lines, which the crew was using to close the safety valves. However, the blowout preventer did not work. The entire sequence of activity led to the explosion that destroyed the Deepwater Horizon oil rig.

borehole: a deep, narrow hole made in the ground, especially to locate water or oil

DIY

Prepare a short report on the 1991 Gulf War Oil Spill.

You can include following information in your report.

1. Location of the oil spill
2. Causes of oil spill
3. Impacts of the oil spill
4. Cleaning of the oil spill

Impacts of the Oil Spill

The oil flowed from the rig for 87 days and the spill covered an area of almost 1,80,000 square kilometres. The oil from the rig spread to the coastlines of Louisiana, Mississippi, Florida and Alabama.

Impact on marine life

The area affected by the oil spill was home to 8,332 marine species, comprising fish, birds, octopuses, sea turtles and marine mammals. This spill harmed around 39 marine species, which is a threat to the marine ecology. The impact on the corals was devastating. Scientists have found evidence of widespread damage of the corals deep in the sea. Some of these corals were more than 600 years old. They have a slow growth rate and longevity, which makes them extremely vulnerable and slow to recover from any adversity. Rhodoliths are rich seaweed assemblages. These provide habitat for deep-sea shrimps, crabs and lobsters. Many of these rodoliths died after the oil spill. The oil spill also affected many marine mammals. It is estimated that nearly 170 marine mammals died. The oil spill caused life threatening diseases and many deaths. The bottlenose dolphins exposed to oil were afflicted with moderate to severe lung disease. More than 1000 sea turtles were found dead in the oil spill. Marine birds including seagulls, pelicans, roseate spoonbills, egrets, terns and blue heron were affected by the spill.

Impacts on estuarine

The estuarine habitats of the Gulf of Mexico were affected greatly. Shallow water sediments and sea grass that provide food and shelter were destroyed in the oil spill.

Economic impact

We have already learnt that any disaster affects the economic life adversely. The economic setbacks are faced by both communities and individuals. The Gulf is one of the richest fishing grounds, however, after this incident, the commercial fishing industry faced a huge loss. The tourism industry was also impacted. Hotels in Louisiana, Alabama and Mississippi suffered heavy losses as bookings significantly declined.

estuarine: related to an estuary

Mitigation

Water-oil separation

Hundreds of workers were deployed to separate oil from water. Oil separation is done manually and is more effective in water bodies with less undercurrent. The Gulf has a strong undercurrent, which made cleaning by this method difficult.

Cleaning an oil spill

Controlled burning or in situ burning (ISB)

It is a technique of responding to an oil spill. This involves the controlled burning of oil that has spilled from a vessel, at the location of the spill. It significantly reduces the amount of oil on the water and minimizes the adverse effects of the oil on the environment.

Chemical dispersants

Dispersants are chemicals that break oil slick into very small droplets. They are sprayed onto the spills by specially equipped boats or planes. Dispersants are one of the several tools available to combat oil spills.

Bioremediation

The naturally occurring microbes that can be used to process crude oil are known to exist in the ocean. Bioremediation is a process that utilizes bacteria, fungi and green plants to naturally remove the contaminations.

Geo Connect

Oil spills can also happen when tankers carrying oil collide. Such a disaster occurred in August, 2006 in the Indian Ocean. A Japanese tanker spilled about 1.4 million gallons of crude oil into the Indian Ocean as it collided with a cargo ship.

In a Nutshell

- The Deepwater Horizon oil rig was located in the Gulf of Mexico near the Mississippi river delta in the United States. It was one of the worst oil spills in the history of the world.
- Construction material, a fault in the valve, misinterpretation of pressure data, delayed response, are some of the causes of the disaster.

- The area affected by the oil spill was home to 8,332 marine species, comprising fish, birds, octopuses, sea turtles and marine mammals. This spill harmed around 39 marine species, which is a threat to the marine ecology.
- Shallow water sediments and sea grass that provide food and shelter in estuarine habitats were destroyed in the oil spill.
- This oil spill gravely affected the economy adversely in the regions around the Gulf of Mexico.
- Methods used for mitigation were water-oil separation, controlled burning, chemical dispersants and bioremediation.

Workout

A. Fill in the blanks.

1. .... refers to the release of liquid petroleum into the seas and oceans.
2. An oil spill is a .... disaster.
3. Deepwater Horizon oil spill occurred on ....
4. .... is the uncontrolled release of crude oil or gas.
5. .... are rich seaweed assemblages.

B. Fill in the blanks with the correct answers.

1. .... is the largest global oil and gas company.

   a. Bharat Petroleum b. British Petroleum
   c. American Petroleum d. PetroChina

2. A .... is a device attached to a pipe or a tube which controls the flow of a fluid.

   a. valve b. blowout preventers
   c. tube d. propellers

3. The borehole at the bottom of the rig is capped with .... to prevent leakage.

   a. marble b. cement
   c. concrete d. limestone

C. Give reasons for the following.

1. The oil spill of April 20, 2010 is known as Deepwater Horizon Disaster.
2. Oil spills adversely affect the ecosystem and the marine life.
3. It is difficult to clean up oil spills.

D. Answer these questions in detail.

1. What was the cause of the oil spill in the Gulf of Mexico?
2. What are blowout preventers?

3. What was the impact of the Deepwater Horizon oil spill on the marine life?
4. Which methods were employed to clean the Deepwater Horizon oil spill?

Think Box

Why do you think oil spills are difficult to clean?

Picture Study

Look at the picture and answer these questions.

1. How does an oil spill affect marine life?
2. Name two major oil spills other than the Deepwater Horizon oil spill.

Life Skills and Values

Make a campaign plan and design a poster to make tourists aware about the importance of keeping beaches clean.

Enjoy

Make a PowerPoint presentation on how the marine flora and fauna was affected by the Deepwater Horizon oill spill.

Weblinks

For more information, visit
https://www.epa.gov/enforcement/deepwater-horizon-bp-gulf-mexico-oil-spill
Last accessed on 31/July/2020

Across the Boundary 3

- How Are Most Earthquakes Caused?

The crust of the Earth is not a solid piece. It is more like a puzzle with many pieces. Each piece of the Earth's crust is called a 'plate' or tectonic plate. These plates move constantly. Most of them move so slowly that we cannot even feel the movement. Sometimes, however, the movement is so powerful that everything on the Earth's surface shakes. Presently, the Earth's crust is divided into many major and minor plates. Most of these plates are named for the continents that are located within them. For example, North American Plate, African Plate and Antarctic Plate. The place where the two plates meet is called a plate boundary.

The tectonic plates move in several ways. When the plates move into one another or crash with each other, they form convergent boundaries. When the plates move apart, they form a divergent boundary and when plates move sideways or brush against each other, they form transform boundaries. These movements cause most of the earthquakes on the Earth. Some of them have caused destruction on a huge scale.

- With respect to plate boundaries, find out the answers for these questions.

1. During the 2010 Haiti Earthquake, the movement of which plate was thought to be the initial reason for the earthquake?
2. The converging movement of which two plates is responsible for the uplift of the Himalayan Mountain Range?
3. Which transform fault forms the boundary between the Pacific and the North American Plate?
4. Name a landform that is caused by the divergent movement of the plates.

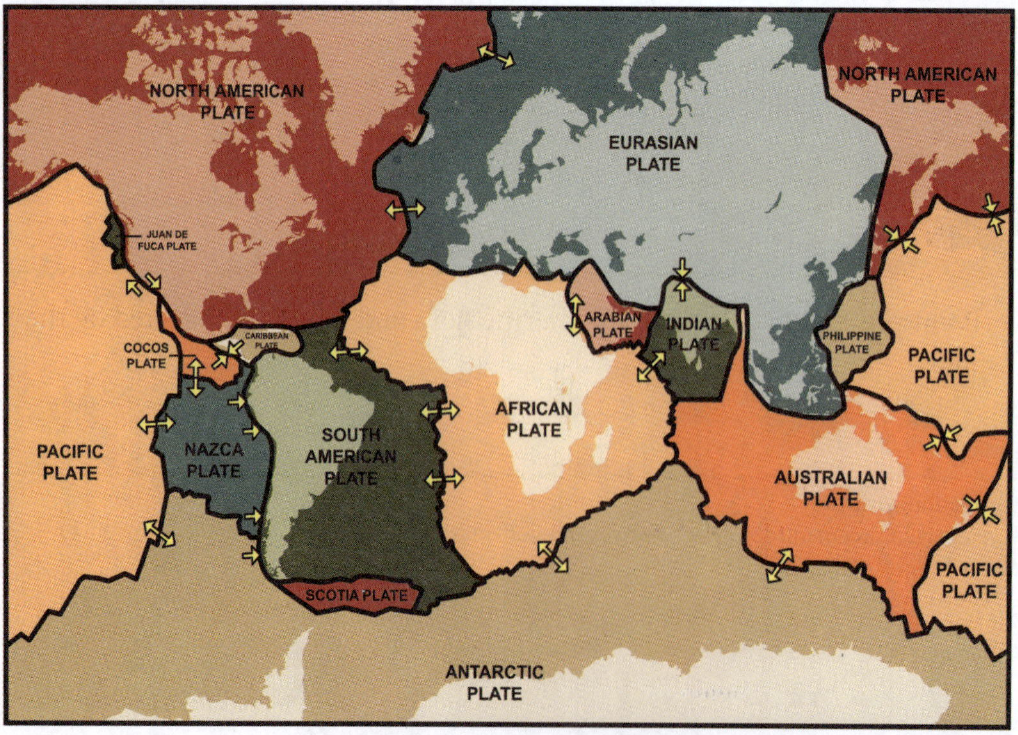

Theme 4

Regional Geography

Regional geography is the study of the relief of a region or country. It helps us analyze the available resources corresponding to the relief and climate. The subject aims at understanding the interaction of the natural environment of a specific region with human communities. Regional geography explores the distinct characteristics of a region. It studies the distribution of plant and animal life, land features, climate and development of human communities in a particular region. In the following chapters, we will learn that Asia was the cradle for most of the ancient civilizations. The great size of this continent made it possible for different civilizations to flourish. Similarly, India is a land of contrast but still a well knit geographical unit. Let us learn more about our country and our continent.

11 Asia: Location, Physical and Political Features

Let's learn about...

- location and extent of Asia.
- physical divisions of Asia.
- political divisions of Asia.

Key Terms

- Asia
- Continent
- China
- India
- South East Asia
- South Asia

Reflect

Look at the physical map of Asia on your atlas and answer these questions.

1. Name three countries located in Asia.
2. Find out the names of three rivers which flow in Asia.
3. In which part of Asia can you see most of the mountain ranges?

Comprising about 30 per cent of the Earth's land area, Asia is the largest continent in the world. The two most populous countries in the world, China and India, are located in Asia, making it the world's most populous continent. Asia makes up the eastern part of the Eurasian supercontinent. Asia is separated from Europe by the Ural Mountains, the Caucasus Mountains, the Black Sea and the Caspian Sea. The Red Sea separates Asia from the African continent. Asia is bordered by the Arctic Ocean in the north, the Pacific Ocean in the east and the Indian Ocean in the south. The Sinai Peninsula connects Asia with Africa. In the east, the Bering Strait separates Asia from North America.

Location

Asia is located in the northern hemisphere, except for a few islands of the Indonesian archipelago, which are in the southern hemisphere. It lies between latitudes 10°S to 80°N and longitude 25°E and 170°W. Asia lies almost entirely in the eastern hemisphere except for a few parts of Asian Russia* that are located in the western hemisphere.

Green Earth

Deforestation and black carbon emissions in Asia are important causes of global warming. Energy demand in Asia is expected to explode with ongoing economic expansion and so will coal use and greenhouse gas emissions.

Eurasian supercontinent: the combined landmass of Europe and Asia

*The eastern part of Russia is a part of Asia, while the western part is a part of Europe.

Physical Divisions of Asia

Asia can be divided into five major physical divisions—the Northern Lowlands, the Central Mountains, the Southern Plateaus, the Great River Valleys and the Islands.

> **FactPedia**
> Japan is an arch-shaped island country comprising nearly four thousand islands. The four major islands are Hokkaido, Honshu, Shikoku and Kyushu. The landscape of Japan is marked with many active and dormant volcanoes.

The Northern Lowlands

The northern part of Asia is made up of the world's largest continuous lowland called the Northern Lowlands. The western part of this lowland is called the West Siberian Plain. This stretch of low-lying land extends from the Ural Mountains in the west to the Bering Strait in the northeast and from the Arctic Ocean in the north to the Central Mountains in the south. This region contains a majority of the world's swamps and floodplains. This is because most of the rivers in this region are frozen at their mouths. These lowlands are triangular in shape and widest in the west. The northern lowlands are drained by three long rivers—the Ob, the Yenisei and the Lena. To the south of the West Siberian Plain is the Turin Plain. It is drained by the rivers Amu Darya and Syr Darya, both of which flow into the Aral Sea.

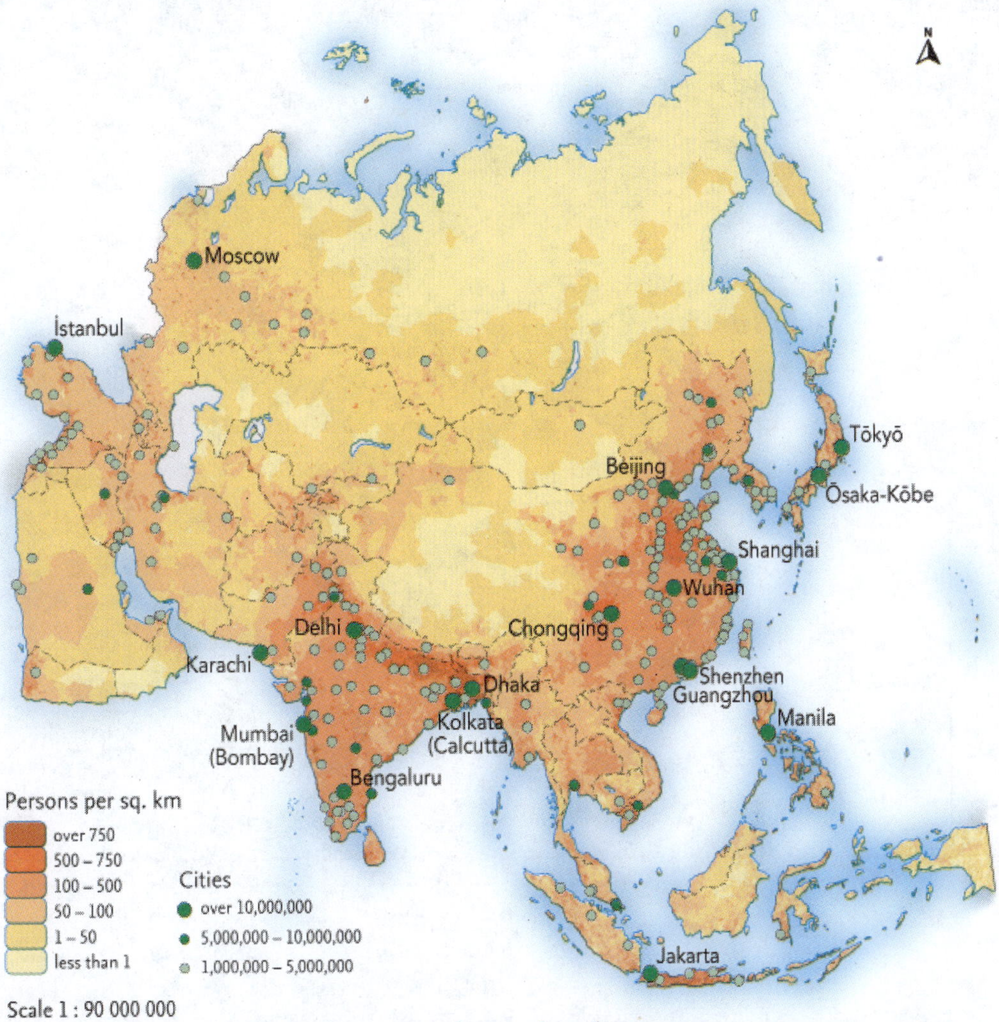

Asia: Population distribution

floodplain: an area of flat land beside a river that regularly becomes flooded when there is too much water in the river

Asia: Physical

The Central Mountains and Plateaus

Alamut, Elburz Mountains, Iran

In the central part of Asia lie a complex system of fold mountain ranges and inter-montane plateaus. These fold mountain ranges appear to radiate in different directions from a single point called the Pamir Knot, which is located near Tajikistan in Central Asia.

To the east and north of the Pamir Knot, extend the Kunlun and Tien Shan mountains, respectively. The Himalayas emerge from the Pamir Knot and then extend towards the southeast in an arc-like shape along the northern extent of India. They turn southwards into Myanmar as the Arakan Yoma Range. The Karakoram Range extends towards the southeast between Kunlun and Himalayan mountain ranges. The Plateau of Tibet, also known as Tibetan Highland, is located between the Kunlun Mountains, Himalayas and Karakoram Ranges. To the west of the Pamir Knot lies the Hindu Kush Range. The Hindu Kush extends into northern Iran, where it is known as the Elburz Mountain Range. A low mountain range, the Sulaiman Range, extends southwest into Pakistan. The westernmost extensions of these mountains extend into Turkey, where they form the Taurus Mountains in the south and the Pontic Mountains in the north.

The Plateau of Anatolia lies between the Pontic and Taurus mountains. It is bounded by the Black Sea in the north, the Caucasus in the northeast, the Aegean Sea in the west, the Iranian Plateau in the east and the Mediterranian Sea in the south. It is roughly a rectangular peninsula that creates a natural bridge between Europe and Asia. Historically, it was known as Asia Minor. The Plateau of Anatolia forms the westernmost, protruding part of Asia and makes up a major part of modern-day Turkey. The Sulaiman Range radiates south-westward from the Pamir Knot and continues as the Kirthar and Zagros ranges. These mountains enclose the Iranian Plateau and converge at the Armenian Knot.

Figure Out

Name the two highest peaks of the Tien Shan mountains.

Southern Plateaus

The Southern Plateaus of Asia are located at the south of the Central Mountains. The central plateau on the Arabian peninsula, the Deccan Plateau and the Yunnan-Guizhou Plateau are the major plateaus of southern Asia. The surface of these plateaus are undulating with a slight slope. They are made of hard crystalline rocks.

The central plateau on the Arabian peninsula is a dry plateau with no rivers flowing through it. The plateau is steeper in the west but gently slopes eastward towards the Persian Gulf. The region

inter-montane plateaus: plateaus that are located in the middle of mountain ranges; Caucasus: the region on the border of Europe and Asia, situated between the Black Sea and the Caspian Sea. Some of the countries include Armenia, Azerbaijan, Georgia, Russia and Turkey

receives low rainfall. The Deccan Plateau is located between the Eastern and the Western Ghats of India. It is steeper in the west along the Arabian Sea and slopes gently in the east along the Bay of Bengal. The Yunnan–Guizhou Plateau is located in China. It is drained by the rivers Salween, Mekong and Si Kiang.

The Mongolian Plateau is located in East Asia. It is surrounded by Tien Shan and the Altai mountains on the west and the north, respectively. Some parts of the Mongolian Plateau form a part of the Gobi Desert.

Gobi Desert

DIY

Find out this information about Asia.

1. Latitudinal extent: ....
2. Longitudinal extent: ....
3. Number of countries: ....
4. Highest elevation: ....
5. Lowest point: ....
6. Largest country: ....
7. Smallest country: ....
8. Longest strait: ....

Great River Basins

Asia is drained by many large rivers that mostly originate from the Central Mountains. These rivers bring sediments from the mountainous regions and deposit them in the plains in the form of alluvial deposits. Most of these rivers are perennial.

The Yangtze River (6,300 km) that flows through the eastern plain of China is the longest river in Asia. The other important rivers flowing through eastern China are the Huang Ho (Yellow River) and the Zhujiang (Pearl River).

In Southeast Asia, Mekong, Salween and Irrawaddy are the main rivers that form large plains. The Mekong river originates in the Yunnan province of China. It flows southward, forming the border between Myanmar and Laos. It flows through Cambodia and southern Vietnam before emptying into the South China Sea.

The Golden Triangle, Mekong River

The major rivers of South Asia originate in the Himalayas. The Ganga originates in the western Himalayas and flows eastward through India. It joins the Brahmaputra River, which originates in Tibet. The Ganga and Brahmaputra flow into the Bay of Bengal. Both the rivers form the largest delta in the world called the Sundarbans, located in India and Bangladesh. The Indus River and its tributaries originate from the western Himalayas and flow through India and Pakistan into the Arabian Sea.

In Southwest Asia, the Tigris and Euphrates are the main rivers which flow into the Persian Gulf. The Mesopotamian Basin lies between these two rivers.

The Ob, Yenisei and Lena are the three longest rivers in Russia. These rivers originate from southern Siberia and form large basins in the regions, through which they flow. The rivers flow northwards and into the Arctic Ocean.

All the river basins of Asia are extremely fertile and are used extensively for agriculture. The Indus-Ganga-Brahmaputra basin and the Yangtze-Huang Ho basin are some of the most densely-populated regions in the world.

The Euphrates flowing through Dura-Europos, Syria

Islands

The islands of Asia are part of the fold mountains and volcanic mountains, mainly concentrated to the east and southeast of the mainland. The islands form large archipelagos in the Pacific Ocean and extend from northeast to the southeast in the form of an arc. The prominent islands from the north to the south are the Kuril Islands, the Japanese Islands, Ryukyu Islands and the Malaya Archipelago (Philippines and the Indonesian Islands). Other important islands are Sri Lanka, Andaman and Nicobar Islands, Lakshadweep Islands and the Maldives that lie in the Indian Ocean in South Asia. Most of the islands have narrow coastal plains and mountainous interiors.

Busuanga Island, Philippines

Political Divisions of Asia	
East Asia	Taiwan, China, North Korea and South Korea, Japan
Southeast Asia	Malaysia, Singapore, Cambodia, Vietnam, Laos, Indonesia, Philippines, Thailand, Brunei, Cambodia, East Timor
South Asia	India, Pakistan, Bangladesh, Nepal, Bhutan, Sri Lanka, Maldives
Middle East	Bahrain, Cyprus, Iran, Iraq, Israel, Jordan, Kuwait, Lebanon, Oman, Qatar, Saudi Arabia, Syria, Turkey, UAE, Yemen
Central Asia	Kazakhstan, Kyrgyzstan, Tajikistan, Uzbekistan, Afghanistan, Turkmenistan, Georgia
Southwest Asia	Saudi Arabia, Yemen, Oman, Bahrain, United Arab Emirates, Kuwait, Iran, Iraq, Jordan, Syria, Israel, Lebanon, Cyprus, Turkey
North Asia	Russia

Countries

Asia: Political

Geo Connect

The Andes is the highest mountain range located in South America. The highest point is Aconcagua. It extends over seven countries namely, Argentina, Bolivia, Chile, Colombia, Ecuador, Peru and Venezuela. It is formed due to subduction of the Nazca plate beneath the South American plate. Like the Himalayas, it is also a young fold mountain.

In a Nutshell

- Asia makes up the eastern part of the Eurasian supercontinent.
- Asia is located in the northern hemisphere, except for a few islands of the Indonesian archipelago, which are in the southern hemisphere.
- Asia can be divided into five major physical divisions—the northern lowlands, the central mountains, the southern plateaus, the great river valleys and the islands.

Workout

A. Fill in the blanks.

1. The Southern Plateau is made of hard .... rocks.
2. The .... river originates in the Yunnan province of China.
3. The Mongolian Plateau is located in .... Asia.
4. Asia is the .... continent and covers .... of the total land area.
5. The Northern Lowlands are drained by the ...., ... and ....

B. Choose the correct answer.

1. Georgia is a country in ....
   a. Central Asia
   b. South Asia
   c. East Asia
   d. Southeast Asia
2. The .... is located between the Eastern and the Western Ghats of India.
   a. Tibetan Plateau
   b. Plateau of Mongolia
   c. Plateau of Anatolia
   d. Deccan Plateau
3. The Arctic Ocean lies to the .... of Asia.
   a. east
   b. west
   c. north
   d. south
4. The Northern Lowlands consist of the West Siberian Plain and ....
   a. Coastal plain
   b. East Siberian Plain
   c. Turan Plain
   d. None of the above

C. Name the following.

1. Pearl of the east ....
2. An ancient civilization in Asia ....
3. The highest volcano in the world ....
4. The longest river in Asia ....
5. A mountain range that separates Asia from Europe ....

D. Give reasons for the following.

1. The Great River Basin is thickly populated.
2. The Ob-Yenisei-Lena river basin plain is a swampy region.
3. The plateau of Anatolia is known as Asia Minor.

E. Complete the following table.

Political division	Any four countries
East Asia	
Southeast Asia	
South Asia	
Southwest Asia	
Central Asia	
North Asia	

F. Answer these questions in brief.

1. State the latitudinal and longitudinal extent of Asia.
2. Define an inter-montane plateau with examples.
3. Where are the following located with reference to Asia?
   a. Mekong river
   b. Ural Mountains
   c. Indian Ocean
   d. Plateau of Mongolia
   e. Tibetan Plateau
4. Trace the path taken by river Mekong in Asia.

G. Write short notes on the following.

1. The Central Mountain System
2. The Northern Lowlands

H. Map Work

On an outline map of Asia, mark the following:

a. Water bodies: Lena, Indus, Mekong, Ob, Yangtze, Aral Sea, Lake Baikal
b. Mountain ranges: Tian Shan, Kunlun, Altai, Western Ghats, Sulaiman
c. Gulfs: Persian Gulf, Gulf of Oman, Gulf of Aden, Gulf of Thailand
d. Plateaus: Tibetan Plateau, Central Siberian Plateau, Deccan Plateau

Think Box

Name two tropical deserts and two temperate deserts of Asia. How are the climatic conditions in temperate deserts different from those in tropical deserts?

Picture Study

Look at the picture and answer these questions.

1. This is a picture of the Mekong river. Through which countries does the river flow?
2. What is the importance of the Mekong river.

Life Skills and Values

The Himalayan region is the source of some of the biggest rivers in India. Find out why the glaciers in the Himalayas are melting at an alarming rate. Suggest ways in which this can be prevented.

Enjoy

Work in groups. Make a list of ten famous tourist destinations of Asia. Collect pictures for each destination and make tourist brochures. You can add important information such as landmarks and things to do.

Weblinks

For more information, visit
https://www.nationalgeographic.org/encyclopedia/asia/
Last accessed on 31/July/2020

12 Asia: Climate, Natural Vegetation and Wildlife

Let's learn about...

- the climate of Asia.
- the natural vegetation of Asia.
- the wildlife of Asia.

Key Terms

- climate
- vegetation
- monsoon
- equatorial climate
- tropical monsoon climate

Reflect

The Gobi Desert is a cold desert in Asia. Temperature in this region is about 40°C in the summer and as low as −40°C in the winter. It has one of the most extreme temperatures in the world. Monsoon is the most stellar climatic feature of South Asia. It brings torrential rainfall from May to September, while some regions are dominated by hot and humid climate.

After reading this, what can you conclude about the climate of Asia? How would you describe the climate of Asia in one word?

Asia is a vast continent. Its latitudinal and longitudinal extent spans across the torrid, temperate and the frigid zones of the Earth. It experiences a varied climate because of the presence of many mountain ranges and inland depressions. In the south, the climate is tropical, ranging from hot to wet. In the north, the climate is extremely cold and dry. In the mid-latitudes, Asia experiences both tropical and temperate climate. The central regions of Asia experience extreme climate and low rainfall due to the lack of moderating influence of the sea.

Factors affecting the climate of Asia

- The northern regions of Asia are exposed to cold Arctic air. Temperature is extreme in these places as they do not experience the warming effect of the maritime climate of the south. The Himalayas form a natural barrier between the north and the south, preventing the cold air from reaching South Asia and moisture-rich air from reaching the freezing north.

The Himalayas act as a natural barrier from the cold Arctic winds

maritime climate: climate experienced in the coastal areas

- The air coming from the Atlantic Ocean loses most of its moisture above Europe and Africa. The air that reaches Asia is continental, with less moisture. Air absorbs moisture over the Pacific Ocean. However, the isolating effect created by the mountain ranges limits the impact of this air on the eastern regions of Asia.
- The monsoon winds are the most spectacular feature of the climate of Asia. These seasonal winds affect a large part of Asia, especially the Indian subcontinent. They are caused by the asymmetrical heating of land and sea. They blow onshore during the summer and offshore during the winter. The cold and warm ocean currents also influence the climate of India.

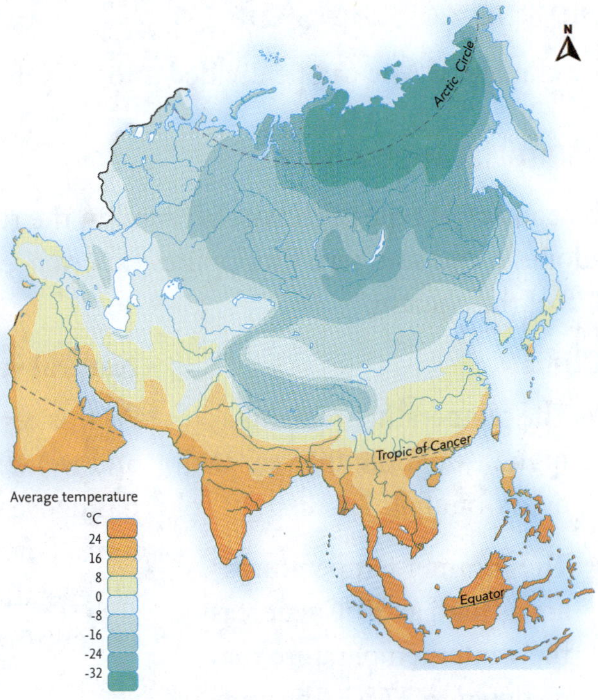

Asia temperature, January

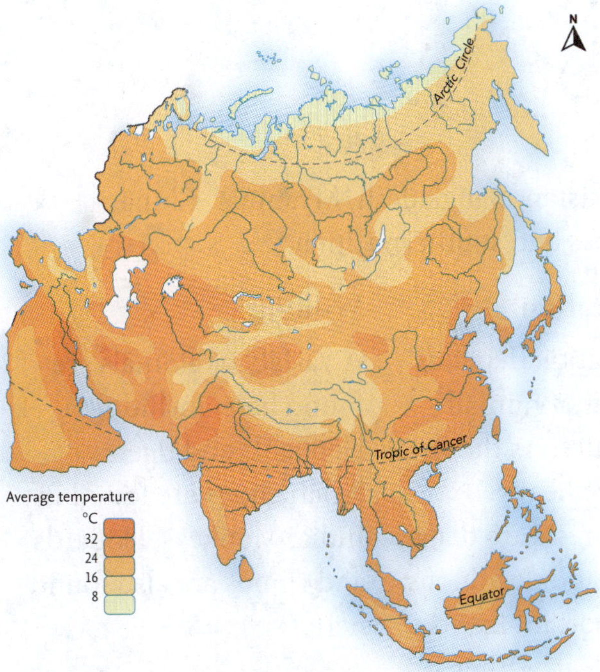

Asia Temperature: July

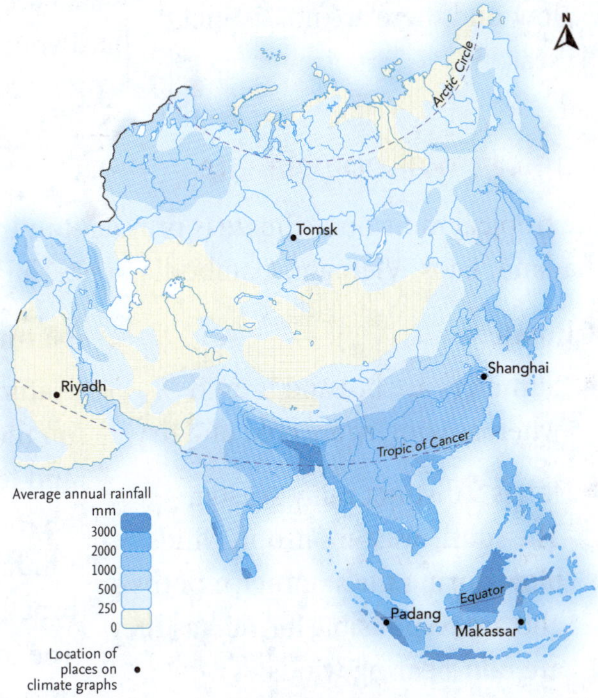

Asia: Annual rainfall

FactPedia

The cold Oyashio current and the warm Kuroshio current influence the climate of East Asia. The Oyashio current, which originates in the north and blows over the western coast of Japan, affects the climate of the country by making it extremely cold. The east coast of Japan receives the warm Kuroshio current that makes the winters milder.

Climatic Zones of Asia

The climate of Asia can be divided into the following categories:

Equatorial-type climate

The equatorial type of climate is found in the regions located close to the equator. Malaysia, Indonesia and southern Philippines experience this climate as they are located between 10°N and 10°S of the equator.

Climate	Natural vegetation	Wildlife
▪ The temperature remains high throughout the year with heavy rainfall. ▪ The summer temperatures are as high as 30°C whereas the winter temperature may go down to 27 °C. The annual range of temperature is very low, and there are no distinct seasons.	As this region experiences hot and wet climate, it, therefore, has dense vegetation. The forest cover has a wide variety of vegetation and thick undergrowth of shrubs and creepers. The main trees are mahogany, ebony and rosewood, which are broad-leaved hardwood trees.	This region has thick dense undergrowth, making it difficult for ground animals to survive. Thus, most of the animals that live on the trees like monkeys, tree lizards, tree frogs, snakes and sloths are found here.

Tropical monsoon climate

The tropical monsoon climate is prevalent in India, Pakistan, Bangladesh, Myanmar, China, Thailand, Laos, Vietnam, Cambodia, western Philippines and southern China.

Climate	Natural vegetation	Wildlife
▪ Summers are hot and humid whereas winters are cold and dry. ▪ It has a distinct rainy season. The south-west monsoon winds blow during the summer months and are responsible for rain as they are rain-bearing winds. ▪ Places near the coast and windward side of the mountains receive more rainfall than the interior region and the leeward side of the mountain. During the winter, this region is under the influence of cold dry winds.	Natural vegetation depends on the amount of rainfall and temperature. As these regions receive heavy rainfall, the forests are dense, broad-leaved and deciduous. The most important tree of this region is teak. Other trees are Sal, rosewood, deodar and bamboo.	A variety of animals are found here, including elephants and tigers. Asiatic lions are found in India. Monkeys, leopards and rhinos are also found here.

FactPedia

The panda, the tiger and the orangutan are the three most endangered animals in Asia. China's forest reserves have some of the last panda habitats of the world. India is trying its best to conserve the Royal Bengal tiger. The orangutan is safe in the less commercialized rainforests of Borneo and Sumatra.

Asiatic Lion

Tropical desert climate

Tropical deserts that are found in Asia are the Arabian Desert in Saudi Arabia and the Thar Desert in India.

Climate	Natural vegetation	Wildlife
▪ Winters are cool and summers are hot with very little rainfall. ▪ The difference between day and night temperatures is much greater than the difference between summer and winter temperatures.	The hot and dry conditions allow very little vegetation to grow. Plants that mostly grow in the region are cactus, thorny bushes and shrubs. These plants have roots that spread far and wide to absorb the sub-surface water. These plants are modified to obtain and conserve water in different ways.	Mainly burrow animals like scorpions, gazelles, mules and horses are found in this region. The camel is the most important animal and is known as the ship of the desert. It has the ability to go without water for many days.

Mediterranean climate

The Mediterranean-type of climate is found in the countries bordering the Mediterranean Sea—Turkey, Syria, Lebanon, Israel and west Asia.

Climate	Natural vegetation	Wildlife
▪ Summers are hot and dry, and winters are mild and wet. ▪ They receive mild rainfall in winter.	Plants have adapted in order to survive long hot summers. They have long roots, waxy leaves, thick spongy barks. Fruits grow well here. Evergreen laurel and acacia are grown here.	Domesticated animals, such as donkeys, cattle and sheep inhabit this region.

Temperate grassland or steppe climate

The steppe climate is prevalent in eastern Mongolia and regions around the Caspian Sea, especially, Kazakhstan and Uzbekistan.

Tash Rabat, a dry grass mountain valley in Kyrgyzstan

Climate	Natural vegetation	Wildlife
■ Winters are very cold, and summers are warm. Annual range of temperature is high. ■ Scanty rainfall is experienced during early summers.	Rainfall is not sufficient for trees to grow so this region has a vast stretch of mountains	Antelopes, mules, horses and wolves are found in the steppes.

Temperate or latitude desert climate

Temperate or mid-latitude type of climate is prevalent in the Gobi Desert and in the Tibetan Plateau.

Climate	Natural vegetation	Wildlife
■ Summers are very hot with very little rainfall. ■ Winters are very cold and the temperature remains below freezing point for several months.	The land is mostly barren and wind swept. Thus, the vegetation is very scanty and consists of scattered tufts of coarse grass and shrubs.	Wildlife mostly includes rodents, lizards and small insects.

China-type or the cool temperate eastern margin climate

This type of climate is prevalent in central and eastern China, southern Japan, and South and North Korea.

Figure Out

Why do the Japanese refer to typhoons as a kamikaze or the 'divine wind'?

Climate	Natural vegetation	Wildlife
■ The summers are hot and winters are mild. It receives moderate rainfall. ■ The winds that bring rain are similar to the monsoon winds. ■ It lies in the trade wind belt thus, it receives rainfall in summer.	Mixed forests are found here. The trees are evergreen as the region receives high temperature and heavy rainfall. Oak, camphor, camellia and magnolia trees grow here. Bamboos and Mulberry shrubs also grow here.	Rodents, lizards and small insects are found in regions with this type of climate.

Manchurian-type climate

Manchurian type of climate is found in northeast China in the plains of the Manchuria region and Hokkaido and in the northern islands of Japan.

Climate	Natural vegetation	Wildlife
■ Winters are very cold, and summers are short and warm. ■ Rainfall is moderate and occurs in the summer.	The mountainous region is covered by coniferous forests. Spruce, fir and pine are some of the trees that grow here.	Fur-bearing animals like bears, foxes and squirrels are found here.

Taiga climate

Taiga climate is also called the Siberian type or coniferous type climate. This region stretches in a broad belt through northern Russia and northern Siberia.

Figure Out

Why is permafrost degradation on the rise in parts of Siberia, Central Asia and the Tibetan Plateau?

Climate	Natural vegetation	Wildlife
■ Winters are very cold and severe and lasts for several months, whereas summers are warm and short. ■ Rainfall varies from very little to moderate. Rainy days are experienced mainly in the summer. Most of the precipitation is in the form of snow.	The vegetation consists of coniferous trees, which do not shed their leaves in the winter. Common trees are pine, fir, spruce and cedar.	The animals found here are few and they are mostly fur-bearing animals like mink, sable, lynx and squirrel. Most of the animals survive severe winters by hibernating or migrating.

Tundra climate

The tundra lies beyond the coniferous belt. It is found in the northern parts of Russia.

DIY

Collect pictures of some animals that are endemic to Asia. Paste their pictures in a scrapbook and mark the regions where they are found on an outline map of Asia.

A tundra region

Climate	Natural vegetation	Wildlife
■ This region is known for long severe winters. Summers are short and cold. ■ Rainfall is scanty and mostly in the form of snow.	Vegetation is sparse as the ground remains frozen throughout the year. This kind of frozen sub-soil is called permafrost. Vegetation is in the form of mosses and lichens as they can survive under snow. During summer, the land is bright with flowers. Trees do not grow because the surface is frozen during the winter and the sub-soil remains permanently frozen.	Reindeer is the most important animal in the tundra. Whales, seals and walruses are common. Fish is found in the sea bordering the coast. The Arctic fox, polar bear, musk, ox and sable are commonly found. These animals have a thick fur to keep them warm in the snow.

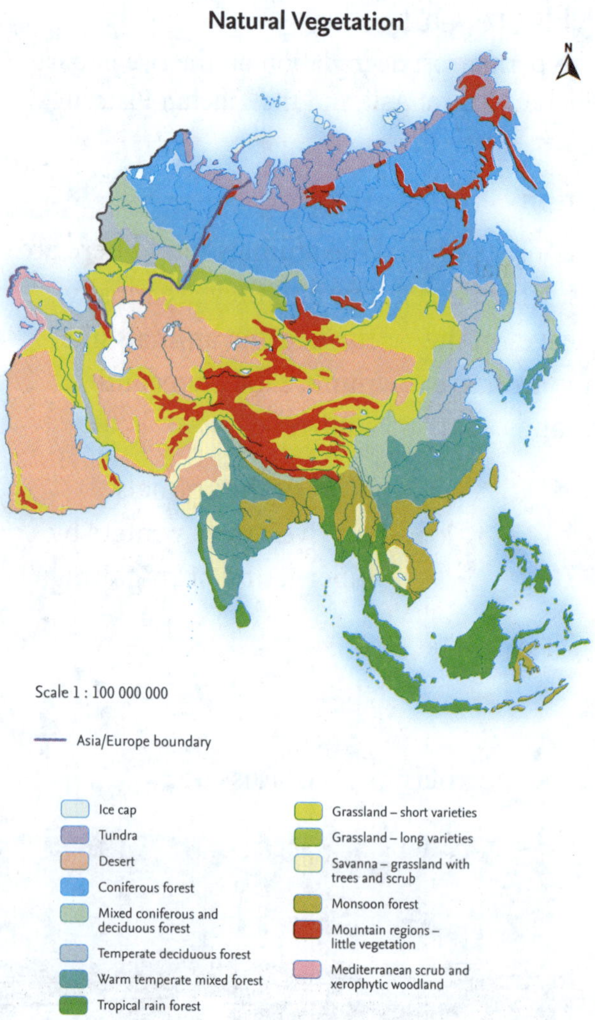

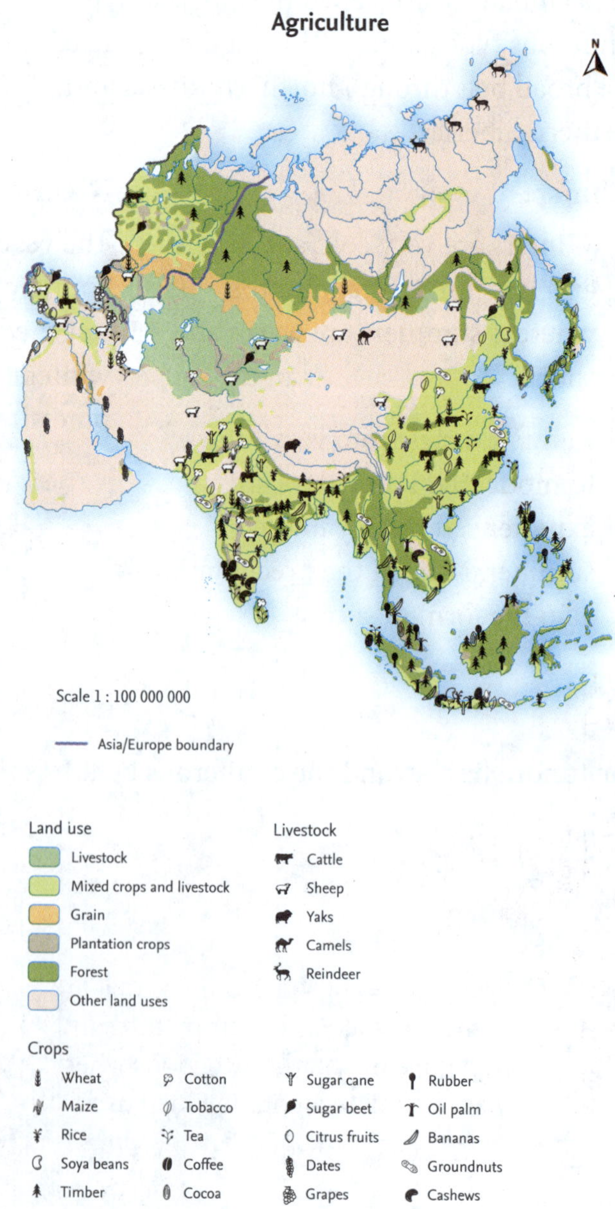

Geo Connect

About 35 per cent of the land area in Europe is covered by forests. In fact, forest cover has increased in the recent years. Europe is a much greener region as it has recovered from deforestation by organized and effective afforestation programmes.

In a Nutshell

- Asia is a vast continent. Its latitudinal and longitudinal extent spans across the torrid, temperate and the frigid zones of the Earth.
- The factors that affect the climate of Asia are the cold Arctic air that blows through the northern regions, the air coming from the Atlantic Ocean and the monsoon winds.
- The climatic zones of Asia are equatorial type climate, tropical monsoon climate, tropical desert climate, Mediterranean climate, temperate grassland climate, temperate desert climate, China-type climate, Manchurian-type climate, taiga climate and tundra climate.

Workout

A. Fill in the blanks.

1. The coniferous belt beyond the tundra is called ....
2. The .... region stretches in a broad belt through northern Russia and northern Siberia.
3. The three most endangered animals of Asia are ...., ... and ....
4. Tropical deserts found in Asia are the .... in Saudi Arabia and the Thar Desert in ....

B. Complete the table.

Climatic Region	Climate	Natural Vegetation	Wildlife
The tundra			
		Citrus fruits	
China-type			
Manchurian-type			

C. Fill in the blanks with the correct answers.

1. Permanently frozen subsoil is also known as ....
   a. permafrost
   b. permanent frost
   c. Both a. and b.
   d. None of the above
2. Antelopes, mules, horses and wolves are found in the ....
   a. downs
   b. steppes
   c. pampas
   d. savanna
3. Asia stretches from the .... to the ....
   a. Antarctic Circle, Northern Hemisphere
   b. Antarctic Circle, Southern Hemisphere
   c. Arctic Circle to, Southern Hemisphere
   d. Arctic Circle, Northern Hemisphere
4. The natural vegetation in the Mediterranean-type of climate includes ....
   a. mahogany and rosewood
   b. mosses and lichens
   c. evergreen laurel and acacia
   d. date palms and cacti

D. Answer these questions in detail.

1. List the factors that determine the climate of Asia.
2. Write a short note on:
   a. Mediterranean type of climate
   b. Equatorial type of climate
3. Explain the difference between the topical desert and the temperate desert climates.
4. How have the plants in tropical desert adapted to the extreme climatic conditions?

E. Map Work

On an outline map of Asia, mark the following:

1. Regions of equatorial climate
2. Regions of Mediterranean climate
3. The steppes
4. Areas affected by monsoon

Think Box

Areas farther from the ocean, for the most part, are dry. Why do Hong Kong and Tokyo experience a humid subtropical climate?

Picture Study

Look at the picture and answer these questions.

1. This is a picture of Ladakh, India. What kind of natural vegetation is found here?
2. Name three wild animals found in Ladakh.

Life Skills and Values

Asia has many tourist places. People from all over the world come to see this amazing continent. Tourism is a source of regular income for many countries in Asia. However, tourism has disturbed the fragile balance of various ecosystems. Create an awareness program and inform people about the damage caused by the tourism industry and how it exploits the local resources of a region.

Enjoy

1. Work in groups. Prepare a PowerPoint presentation on the wildlife of Asia. Collect pictures of some of the unique animals and birds found in this region and present it in the classroom.
2. Work in groups. Make a list of ten famous tourist destinations of Asia. Collect pictures for each destination, and make tourist brochures. You can add important information such as landmarks and activities to do.

Weblinks

For more information, visit
https://www.britannica.com/place/Asia/Plant-life
Last accessed on 31/July/2020

13 India: Political and Physical Features

Let's learn about...

- the location of India.
- the six major physical divisions of India.
- the political divisions of India.

Key Terms

- Himalayas
- islands
- Indian subcontinent
- peninsular plateau

Reflect

We have all been studying about our country right from our childhood. All of us have visited different places, our native village, town or city and tourist spots within the country. Think about them and write one sentence describing those places. It should not be more than ten words. Now share it with your classmates.

India is officially known as the Republic of India. It is a country located in South Asia. India is the seventh largest country and the second most populous country in the world. The Himalayas form a natural barrier between India and the rest of Asia, which has led to the development of a unique cultural and physical identity. India, Pakistan, Bhutan, Nepal, Bangladesh and Sri Lanka together form a subcontinent. India occupies a major part of this subcontinent. The entire region is called the Indian subcontinent.

Location

India lies entirely in the Northern and Eastern hemispheres. It extends from 8°4′ N to 37°6′ N latitudes and 68°7′ E to 97°25′ E longitudes. The Tropic of Cancer (23°30′N) passes through India and divides the country into two parts. The longitude of 82°30′E, is considered to be the standard time meridian of India. It passes through Mirzapur in Uttar Pradesh. The Indian Standard Time (IST) is 5 hours and 30 minutes ahead of the Greenwich Mean Time (GMT).

FactPedia

India's history is connected with the Indus river, from where its present name originated. The Persians referred to the river Sindhu as Hindu. The Greeks called it Indus and gave the land its present name, India.

Neighbouring Countries

India has a long coastline. It shares its borders with Pakistan, China, Nepal, Bhutan, Myanmar, Bangladesh and Afghanistan. There is a small boundary between India and Afghanistan in the northwest part of our country. We share water boundaries with Sri Lanka and Maldives. India occupies a strategic location in Asia, surrounded by seas on three sides. India's maritime trade routes have encouraged trade with the neighbouring countries from ancient times.

Political Divisions

India is divided into 28 states and 8 union territories for administrative purposes. The country was divided into its current political divisions based on many factors such as geography, population, culture and language. The people of India speak different languages and have diverse cultural, religious and ethnic traits. Rajasthan is the largest state and Goa is the smallest state in India. Delhi is one of the union territories of India. It is also referred to as the National Capital Territory (NCT). New Delhi, the national capital, is a part of the NCT.

India, Political

Physical Divisions

India can be divided into six major physical divisions:

- The Northern Mountains
- The Great Northern Plains
- The Peninsular Plateau
- The Coastal Plains
- The Thar Desert
- The Islands

India, Physical

The Northern Mountains

The two main mountain ranges that make up the Northern Mountains are the Karakoram Range and the Himalayas.

The Karakoram Range is a huge mountain range that originates in Central Asia and extends to the southeast along the borders of Tajikistan, China, Pakistan, Afghanistan and India. This mountain range lies between the Pamir Plateau and the Indus Valley. The Karakoram Range has some of the highest mountains in the world. K2, also called Mount Godwin Austen, is the world's second-highest peak and is located in this mountain range. The Baltoro and Siachen glaciers are found in this region.

K2, Karakoram Range

The Himalayas extend from the Indus Valley in the west to the Brahmaputra in the east, stretching for about 2,500 km. The width of this mountain range varies between 150 km and 400 km. The Himalayas are young fold mountains with high peaks, deep gorges and vast glaciers. They are also continuously rising, causing frequent earthquakes and landslides in the region.

Within India, the Himalayas are divided into three parallel ranges on the basis of their heights—the Outer Himalayas, the Lesser Himalayas and the Greater Himalayas.

- The Outer Himalayas form the southernmost range of the Himalayas. They have an average elevation of about 1200 m above the mean sea level. They form the southern-most range of the Himalayas. Interspersed in the Shiwaliks are broad flat longitudinal valleys known as duns. These valleys are heavily populated and vast cultivations are common. Dehra Dun, Patli Dun and Kotli Dun are examples of such valleys.
- The Lesser Himalayas are also called the Lower or Middle Himalayas. They lie to the north of the Shiwalik Range. The average elevation of this range is 4500 m above the mean sea level. Kashmir, Kangra and Kullu are located in this region. Some of the hill stations located here are Shimla, Mussoorie, Ranikhet, Nainital and Darjeeling.

Figure Out

Name the glaciers and mountain passes that are located in the Himalayan mountain range.

- The Greater Himalayas are also known as the Inner Himalayas, the Great Himalayas or Himadri. The average elevation of the mountains is 6,000 m above the mean sea level. Some of the highest peaks in the world belong to the Greater Himalayas. Mount Everest (8,848 m) is located on the China-Nepal border. Kanchenjunga (8,586 m), which is the highest point in India, is located on the border of Nepal and Sikkim.

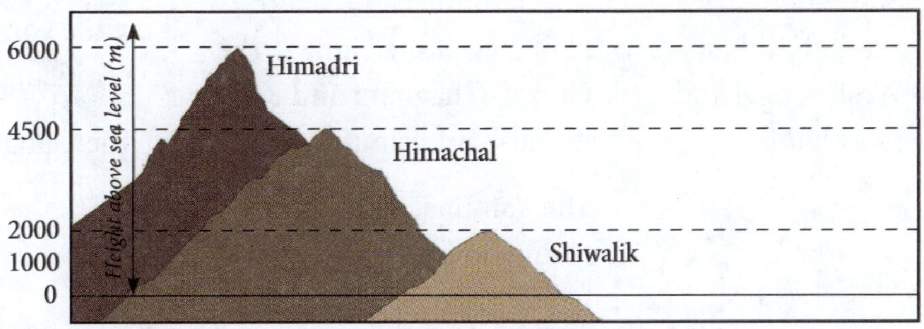

- A number of ranges and hills run parallel to the Himalayas. The Zanskar and Ladakh ranges are located in Ladakh. They extend to the northeast of the Greater Himalayas. The Pir Panjal Range, also in Jammu and Kashmir, extends to the southwest of the Great Himalayas.
  The easterly extensions of the Himalayas, beyond the Brahmaputra valley, are collectively known as Purvachal. Patkai, Naga, Garo, Khasi, Jaintia and Mizo Hills are a part of the Purvachal.

The Great Northern Plains

The Great Northern Plains are located at the foothills of the Lesser Himalayas. They extend from Punjab in the west to the Brahmaputra valley in the east. The land is flat and levelled with minute undulation. Composed of the fertile alluvium brought down by the perennial rivers of this region, this plain is formed due to the depositional activity of the three major rivers of India—the Indus, the Ganga and the Brahmaputra.

The Great Northern Plains can be divided into three parts from west to east—the Indus river basin, the Ganga river basin and the Brahmaputra river basin.

Green Earth

Punjab produces about two-thirds of the food grains in India. Farmers use fire to clear fields and get them ready for new crops. Although the fires are not immediately hazardous, such widespread burning can have a detrimental impact on weather, climate, human health and natural resources.

River system	Main rivers and tributaries	Source and mouth of the main river
The Indus river basin **States:** Punjab, Haryana and Himachal Pradesh	This region is drained by the river Indus along with its tributaries—Jhelum, Chenab, Ravi, Beas and Sutlej.	The river Indus originates near lake Manasarovar, which is located near Mount Kailash in the Tibetan Plateau. Most of its tributaries rise from the glaciers in the Karakoram, Ladakh and Zanskar ranges. The Indus flows into the Arabian Sea.
The Ganga river basin **States:** Uttar Pradesh, Bihar, West Bengal and Jharkhand	This region is drained by the Ganga and its tributaries. The Yamuna is the main tributary of the Ganga. The Gomti, Ghaghara and Kosi are its left-bank tributaries. The Yamuna, Son and Damodar are its right-bank tributaries.	The river Ganga originates from the Gangotri Glacier at Gomukh. Most of its tributaries originate in the Himalayas, while some originate at the edge of the Peninsular Plateau. The Ganga flows into the Bay of Bengal.

undulation: a smoothly rising and falling form, outline, or movement

The Brahmaputra river basin **States:** Arunachal Pradesh, Assam and some parts of West Bengal	This region is drained by the river Brahmaputra and its tributaries. The Teesta, Subansiri, Manas and Sankosh are its tributaries.	The Bhramhaputra River originates from the glaciers of the Kailash Range near the Manasarovar lake, also known as lake Mapam.

The Peninsular Plateau

The Peninsular Plateau is also known as the Indian Plateau. It lies to the south of the Vindhya and the Satpura ranges. The plateau begins from Aravalli in the northwest and the region surrounding it is made up of igneous and metamorphic rocks. It is higher in the south and the height decreases northwards. The following flowchart shows the plateaus of the Peninsular Plateau.

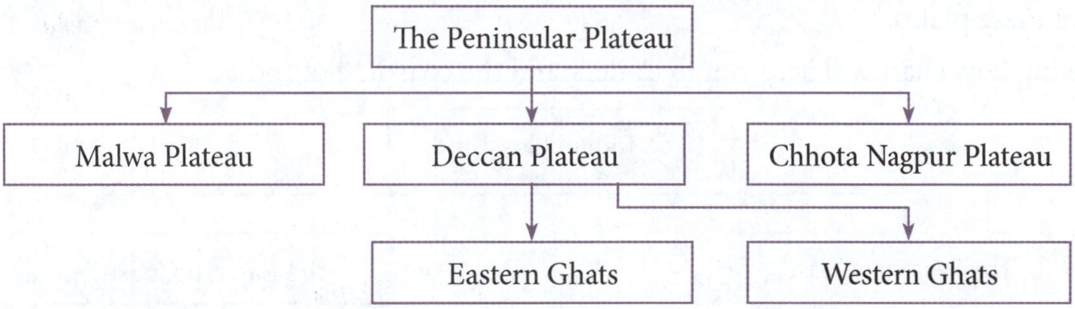

- The Malwa Plateau forms the northern part of the Peninsular Plateau. It is bounded by the Aravalli Range in the west and the Vindhya and Satpura ranges in the south. The plateau comprises central Madhya Pradesh and southeastern Rajasthan. The Mahi, Betwa, Chambal, Parbati, Sipra and Gambhir are some of the rivers that flow through this plateau.
- The Chhota Nagpur Plateau is located in northwestern Chhattisgarh and central Jharkhand. It is higher in the south and its height deceases northwards. The Ranchi Plateau is its largest division. This plateau was formed due to fissure eruption. The plateau is located between the basins of Ganga and Son rivers in the north and on the Mahanadi river in the south.

DIY

Why do rivers tend to flow from the west to the east in the plateau region?

- The Deccan Plateau lies to the south of the Satpura Range. The plateau is bounded on the east and the west by two big escarpments—the Western Ghats and the Eastern Ghats. The Western Ghats are also called Sahyadris. Satmala, Nilgiri, Anaimalai and Cardomom Hills are a few hills that belong to the Sahyadris and in Tamil Nadu they form the Nilgiri hills. Anai Mudi (2,695 m) is the highest peak in South India.

Agastya Mala, Western Ghats

fissure: a deep, narrow crack, especially in rocks or the earth; escarpment: a long, steep slope at the edge of a plateau

The Eastern Ghats are lower than the Western Ghats. The Godavari, Mahanadi, Krishna, Tapi and Kaveri are the principal rivers flowing through this plateau.

The Coastal Plains

The geographical unit that makes the coast of India is referred to as the the coastal plains. They can be divided into the Western Coastal Plains and the Eastern Coastal Plains.

- The Eastern Coastal Plains extend from the Subarnarekha river along the West Bengal-Odisha border to Kanyakumari. They are known as the Northern Circars between the Mahanadi and the Krishna rivers, and Coromandel Coast between the Krishna and the Kaveri rivers.
- The Western Coastal Plains extend from the Kutch in the north to Kanyakumari in the south. Kutch and Kathiawar are a part of these plains.

The Malabar Coast on the Western Coastal Plains.

The following flow chart will help you to understand the coastline of India.

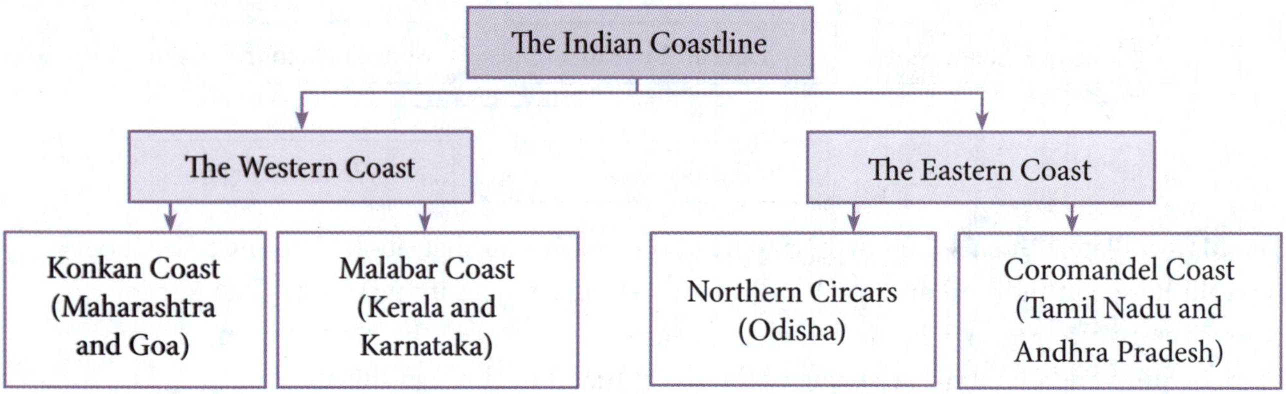

The Thar Desert

The Thar Desert is mostly located in northwestern Rajasthan. It is a low-lying zone of undulating and shifting sand hills, separated by sandy plains and low barren hills. The sand dunes in this region shift from one place to another continuously and take up different shapes and sizes. However, older dunes are relatively more stable. The Luni is the only significant river that exists in this region. Lake Sambhar, a saltwater lake, is found here. The Indira Gandhi Canal, which draws water from the Sutlej, is the main source of water.

The Islands

India has two remarkable group of islands—the Andaman and Nicobar archipelago in the Bay of Bengal and the Lakshadweep islands in the Arabian Sea.

- The Andaman and Nicobar Islands are a group of 324 islands. Most of these islands are uninhabited. Anadaman and Nicobar Islands are seperated by Ten Degree Channel which is a deep sea.

Barren Island on the Andaman Sea is the only active volcano in India

- Three islands, namely, Amindivi, Laccadive and Minicoy, together form the Lakshadweep Islands. They are tiny islands of coral origin surrounded by fringing reefs. They are mostly uninhabited and together form the smallest union territory of India.

Lakshadweep Islands

Geo Connect

Sri Lanka is a neighbouring country of India. Adam's Bridge is a chain made of limestone shoals above the sea level between the Pamban Island in India and the Mannar Island in Sri Lanka. Geologists believe that this bridge was previously a land connection between India and Sri Lanka.

In a Nutshell

- India lies entirely in the northern and the eastern hemispheres.
- India's neighbouring countries are Pakistan, Afghanistan, China, Nepal, Myanmar, Bangladesh, Bhutan, Sri Lanka and Maldives.
- India is divided into 28 states and 8 union territories.
- India can be divided into six main physical divisions—the Northern Mountains, the Great Northern Plains, the Peninsular Plateau, the Coastal Plains, the Thar Desert and the Islands.

Workout

A. Fill in the blanks with the correct answers.

1. Sri Lanka is separated from India by the ....

   a. Palk Strait b. Gulf of Mannar c. Bering Strait d. Isthmus of Suez

2. India is divided into .... states.

   a. 30 b. 27 c. 28 d. 25

3. The eastern extension of the Himalayas is known as ....

   a. Purvanchal b. Uttaranchal c. Pir Panjal d. Himadri

4. The Baltoro and Siachen glaciers are found in the ....

   a. Himalayas b. Karakoram Range
   c. Purvanchal d. Great Northern Plains

B. Write T for true and F for false.

1. India is located in South Asia. ☐
2. India shares its boundaries with Afghanistan. ☐
3. The Ten Degree Channel separates the Andaman Islands from the Nicobar Islands. ☐
4. The Himalayas are divided into five divisions based on their location. ☐
5. Kanchenjunga (8,586 m), which is the highest point in India, is located on the border of India with China. ☐

C. Answer these questions in brief.

1. Explain the location and physical features of the Outer Himalayas.
2. Name the neighbouring countries of India.
3. How were the political divisions in India created?
4. State the location of the Chhota Nagpur Plateau.
5. Explain the physical features of the Peninsular Plateau of India.

D. Answer these questions in detail.

1. Name the physical divisions of India. State any two features of each division.
2. Draw a flowchart showing the various divisions and subdivisions of the Peninsular Plateau.
3. Write a short note on the rivers flowin g through the Northern Plains.
4. Differentiate between the eastern and the western coastal plains.
5. Write a short note on the islands of India.

Think Box

India is a large landmass that was formed during different geological periods. Find out which events led to its formation.

Picture Study

Look at the picture and answer these questions.

1. This is a picture of the Emerald Lake in Ooty. In which mountain range is Ooty located?
2. What kind of climate does Ooty experience?

Life Skills and Values

Write a script for a street play about 'unity in India'. Take the help of your language teacher to write the dialogues.

Enjoy

Make an informative journal about the location of the different states of India. You can place the states under the following groups:

- States of the Himalayan region
- States of the Great Northern Plains
- States that make up the Peninsular Plateau
- States of the coastal plains
- States of northeast India
- States that form the Thar Desert

You can paste pictures from each state to make the journal colourful.

Weblinks

For more information, visit
https://www.india.gov.in/india-glance/profile
Last accessed on 31/July/2020

14 India: Climate, Natural Vegetation and Wildlife

Let's learn about...

- the climate of India.
- the factors influencing the climate of India.
- the types of vegetation in India.
- the wildlife of India.

Key Terms

- monsoon
- hot dry season
- wildlife
- tropical monsoon
- cool dry season
- tropical rainforests

Reflect

Read the passage and answer the questions.

Due to extremely high temperatures and hot weather, summer vacation was extended by a week by the capital's education minister. This order was made in lieu of the heat wave that had gripped Delhi for weeks and is mandatory for all schools including government, government-aided and unaided recognized schools.

1. Discuss how weather influences our lives.
2. Why do you think the government takes such decisions?
3. Is it necessary to reschedule working hours due to such situations?

Climate

In the previous chapter, we read that India has diverse physical and political features. The diversity in the physical features influences the climate of a place. India experiences regional variations in its climate. The coastal areas experience an equable climate, with minor differences in summer and winter temperatures. The interiors of the country experience a continental type of climate, with hot summers and cold winters. For example, Delhi experiences temperatures as low as 5°C during winters and during the same time, Goa experiences a pleasant temperature of about 25°C. There is also a variation between the amounts of rainfall received. For example, Mawsynram in Meghalaya receives heavy rainfall throughout the year, whereas the Thar Desert is bereft of any moisture-rich winds even during the monsoon. Despite these differences, India is said to have a tropical monsoon climate.

Factors Affecting the Climate of India

Latitude

The Tropic of Cancer passes through the middle of India. Therefore, the southern part of India experiences tropical climate as it is close to the Equator. The northern part of India lies in the sub-tropical region and experiences hot summers and cold winters.

Northern mountains

The Himalayan mountain range plays a pivotal role in modifying the climate of India. Firstly, it prevents the cold Arctic winds from entering India during the winter season. Secondly, it does not allow the rain-bearing monsoon winds to leave the country, thus ensuring abundant rainfall.

Altitude

We know that temperature decreases with increasing altitude. Because India has an uneven terrain, the mountainous regions experience lower temperature than the plains. Places located in the Himalayas experience chilling winters. In the Deccan region, places such as Ooty and Kodaikanal also experience cold weather as they are located at a higher elevation from the mean sea level.

A teaplantation in Ooty

Distance from the sea

Places near the coast enjoy equable climate, whereas places located in the interiors have an extreme climate. Nagpur is hotter than Mumbai because the latter is located near the Arabian Sea.

Precipitation

Precipitation also plays an important role in determining climate. The relief influences the amount of precipitation received by a place. The direction of rain-bearing winds determine the amount of rainfall received by a place. The western slopes of the Western Ghats, which lie in the windward side, receive more monsoon rain than the eastern side, which lies in the rain shadow area.

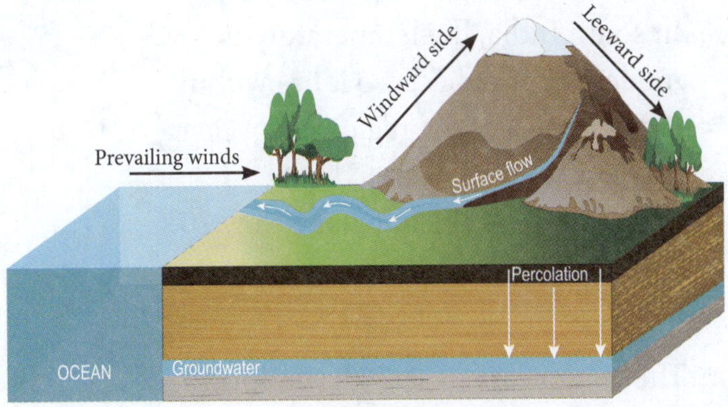

Western disturbances

The low pressure systems that originate over the eastern Mediterranean region in winter visits India in the winter season. These disturbances are responsible for the winter rain in the northern and north western part of India.

pivotal: of great importance because many things depend on it

Jet streams

Air currents in the upper layers of the atmosphere are referred to as jet streams. These are winds with very high speed. These streams determine the arrival and departure of the monsoon winds.

Seasons in India

The tropical monsoon climate of India has four main seasons. They are:

- Cold weather season: December, January, February
- Hot weather season: March, April, May
- South west monsoon: June, July, August, September
- Retreating monsoon: October, November

Green Earth

India is mostly a parched land as the rainfall is concentrated over a few months. Thus, the monsoon commands the need of water conservation. The storage of water for irrigation remains a priority.

Cold weather season

The cold weather season is also called winter or cold dry season. The weather in this season ranges from pleasant to cold.

- When the Sun's vertical rays move south of the Equator, most of the country experiences moderately cool weather. The season begins to set in by November and ends in February. January and December are generally the coldest months.
- In northwest India, the average temperature during winters is low. In south India, the temperature is moderately hot because it lies within the tropics. Coastal regions experience moderate temperature. The mean temperature in the north is below 20°C whereas the mean temperature of the southern part is above 21°C.
- The winters are usually dry in most parts of India. A high-pressure system exists on the land and the winds that are bereft of moisture blow from the land to the sea. However, some rainfall occurs on the Coromandel Coast and in northwest India. The winds that blow over the Bay of Bengal cause rainfall on the east coast of India. These winds are known as the northeast monsoons winds.

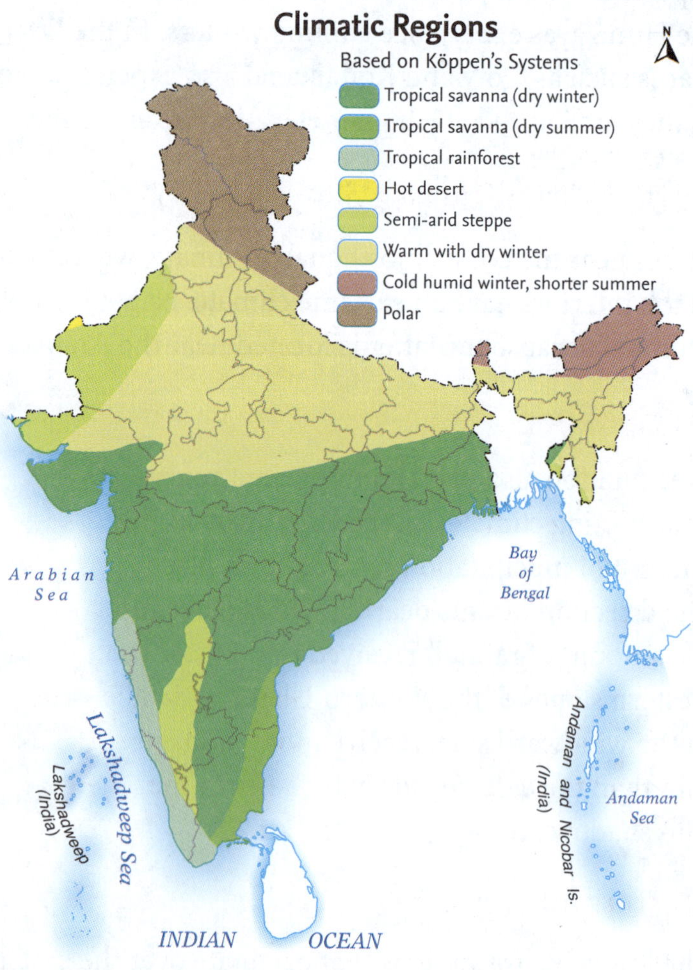

India, Climatic regions

- The northwestern part of India receives rainfall from the western disturbances, which are storms originating in the Mediterranean Sea. They travel eastward across Iran and Pakistan before entering the northwestern part of India. They cause snowfall in the Himalayas and bring rains to the Northern Plains.

The hot weather season

This is also called the summer weather season.

- During this season, India experiences a very high temperature that starts rising from the month of March, reaching its peak in the month of May.

> **FactPedia**
> Rajasthan experiences high temperatures due to sandy soil, direct insolation and no cloud cover.

- A low-pressure area exists over the Thar Desert that extends to the Chhota Nagpur Plateau. The Deccan region experiences slightly high pressure as it is cooler due to the influence of the sea.
- The northern regions develop an intense low-pressure area where the winds are drawn in circulation, resulting in violent thunderstorms and heavy rainfall.

These storms have local names at different places. Kalbaisakhi is experienced in Assam and West Bengal. These are thunderstorms accompanied by strong winds and rainfall. Kalbaisakhi means 'the calamity of the month of Baisakh'. Kalbaisaki, is very beneficial for jute cultivation in West Bengal and tea plantation in Assam. The loo, which is a hot and dry wind, is experienced in the northern part of India, mainly in Bihar, Uttar Pradesh, Punjab and Haryana. It is also known as *andhi*. Mango showers are experienced in Kerala. These rains are good for early ripening of mangoes. They are also important for tea and coffee.

Annual Rainfall and Monsoon

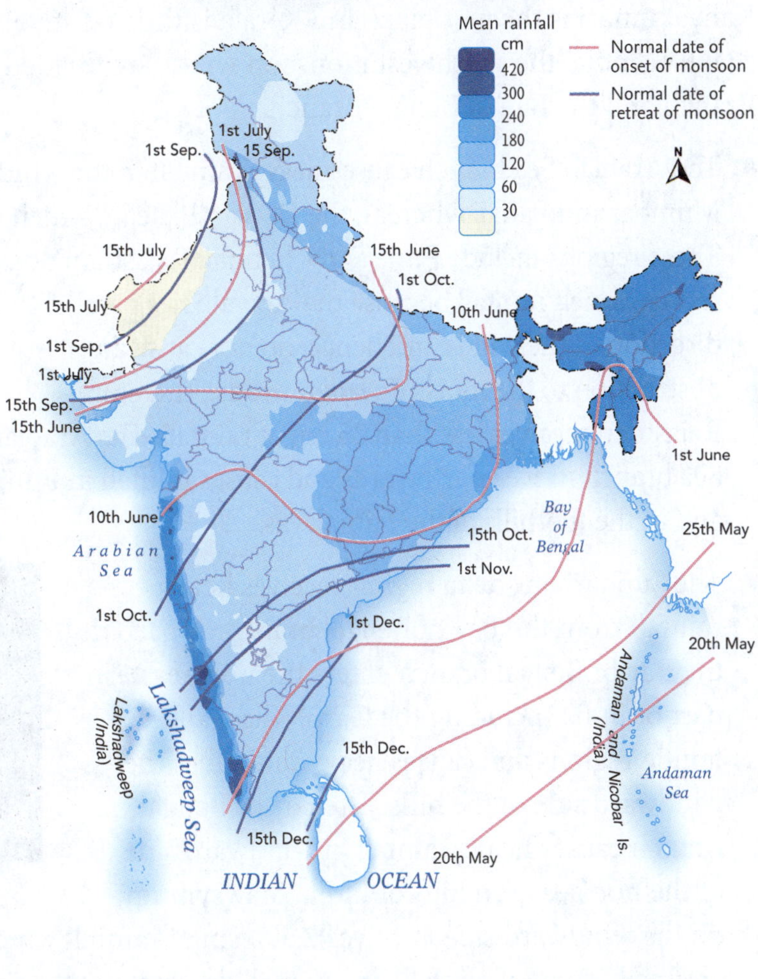

South west monsoon

This is also called the monsoon season or the rainy season. The southwest monsoon is responsible for the bulk of rainfall in India. Monsoon winds originate in the Southern Hemisphere and reach India after crossing the Equator.

Because of excessive heat during the summer season, the land gets heated and a low-pressure area develops in the northern part. Winds blow from high-pressure areas to low-pressure areas.

The southeast trade winds from the Southern Hemisphere enter India as southwest monsoon winds.

The southeast trade winds are the prevailing winds in the Southern Hemisphere. These winds are moisture laden, high-pressure winds. The intense low-pressure trough of the northern plains of India attract these high-pressure winds. These southeast trade winds cross the Equator and deflect to the right due to the coriolis force, and they enter India as the southwest monsoon winds. The onset of monsoon winds is rapid and is caused due to the pressure difference between land and water bodies. They are orographic in nature, thus cause more rainfall in the windward side of the mountain and less rainfall in the leeward side of the mountain.

FactPedia

Burst of monsoon is the sudden approach of the monsoon winds with thunder and lighting.

Break in monsoon is a phenomena related with the monsoon and its tendency to have breaks in rainfall. It refers to wet and dry spells. The monsoon rains are interspersed with rainless intervals.

Approach of monsoon winds

The approach of southwest monsoon winds is sudden, accompanied by thunder and lighting. Kanyakumari is the first place and Kerala is the first state to receive the rain. Due to the triangular shape of India, the southwest monsoon winds are divided into two branches—the Arabian Sea Branch and the Bay of Bengal Branch.

- The Arabian Sea branch causes heavy rainfall in the windward side of the Western Ghats such as, Mumbai and Panaji whereas, the Deccan Plateau, which lies on the leeward side gets less rainfall. These regions include Pune and Chennai. Rajasthan does not receive much rainfall because the Aravalli lies parallel to the direction of the winds and hence, do not cause any obstruction to the moisture laden winds. Therefore, Rajasthan receives less than 25 cm of rainfall. The Arabian Sea branch moves northwards and causes rainfall in Punjab and in the foothills of the Himalayas.

Figure Out

Why does Kodaikanal have a cool climate despite being located in a tropical region?

- The Sundarbans delta region receives heavy rainfall from the Bay of Bengal branch. A part of the Bay of Bengal branch enters the northeastern part of India including the Garo, Khasi and Jaintia regions and causes heavy rainfall in the windward side of the hills. The Bay of Bengal Branch causes heavy rainfall in windward side of the northeastern hills of India. Mawsynram, on the windward side, receives 2,500 cm of rainfall whereas, Shillong, on the leeward side gets around 250 cm of rainfall. The rainfall decreases as the winds move westwards into the Ganga plain.

Khasi Hills, Meghalaya

coriolis force: Due to the Coriolis force winds deflect towards the right in the northern hemisphere and towards the left in the southern hemisphere. This is known as Ferrel's law.

Therefore, Kolkata, which lies in the lower Ganga plain, receives 200 cm of rainfall, Patna, which lies in the middle Ganga plain, receives 150 cm of rainfall and Amritsar, which lies in the upper region, receives 100 cm of rainfall.

Retreating southwest monsoon

The retreating of the southwest monsoon indicates the gradual withdrawal of the monsoon from the Indian mainland. This season is also referred to as the season of transition from a hot, rainy season to a cold, dry winter season. The southwest monsoon withdraws in stages and is referred to as the retreating southwest monsoon.

- We experience this season during the months of October and November.
- The temperature of the northern plain dips due to heavy rainfall. The Sun's rays no longer fall directly on the Tropic of Cancer. During September, the sun shines directly on the Equator and India begins to get cooler.
- During this season, the low pressure of the Indian mainland is slowly replaced by high pressure.
- This season is marked by cyclones in the Bay of Bengal. While withdrawing, the retreating monsoon collects moisture from the Bay of Bengal and causes rainfall in the east coast of India, mainly in Tamil Nadu.

DIY

Collect the daily weather report from the newspaper for a week and complete this table.

Date	Day	Minimum temperature	Maximum temperature	Range	Rainfall

Now, answer these questions.

1. What is the monthly mean temperature? ....
2. Which day was the hottest? ....
3. Which day was the coldest? ....
4. What is the mean monthly rainfall? ....
5. When did it rain the heaviest? ....

Natural Vegetation

We have learnt that India has varied relief, temperature and rainfall. Subsequently, diverse natural vegetation is found across the country. The growth of vegetation depends primarily on temperature and moisture. Two important factors that determine the kind of vegetation are rainfall and relief. On the basis of these two factors, the vegetation of India has been classified into several types.

Based on the variation in rainfall:

- Tropical evergreen forests (found in regions of heavy rainfall)
- Tropical deciduous forests (found in regions of moderate rainfall)
- Thorn and desert forests (found in regions of scanty rainfall)

Based on the variation in relief:

- Tidal forests (found in the delta region of India)
- Montane forests (found in the Himalayan region)

Tropical evergreen forests

Tropical evergreen forests are also called tropical rainforests. The main characteristics of these forests are the evergreen trees that do not shed their leaves throughout the year. These forests are found in regions of heavy rainfall, which receive rainfall between 200 to 300 cm annually. High temperature and humidity is also favourable for the growth of tropical evergreen vegetation. The Andaman and Nicobar Islands, Northeastern hills, windward side of the Western Ghats, parts of Kerala, Odisha and West Bengal have tropical rainforests. The most remarkable feature of tropical rainforests is the presence of tall trees with a thick undergrowth. They are thick forests with climbers, creepers and ferns. The trees in these forests are hardwood trees such as mahogany, rosewood, ebony, shisham, red cedar, teak gurjan and bamboo.

Tropical deciduous forests

Tropical deciduous forests are also called monsoon forests. These forests require an annual rainfall of 100 to 200 cm with a long dry season. The tropical deciduous forests can be tropical moist deciduous forests, which are found in the northern parts of the Eastern Ghats, east-central India and western Karnataka or dry deciduous forests, which are found in Gujarat, Madhya Pradesh, eastern Rajasthan, central Andhra Pradesh and western Tamil Nadu. The trees found in these forests shed leaves only for six to eight weeks during summer, at different times. Therefore, the forests never look barren.

Bandipur National Park in Karnataka

hardwood trees: species of broad-leaved, either perennial or deciduous trees; they are commercially valuable as they yield timber

The tropical deciduous forests are economically the most important forest cover in India. Sandalwood, sal, teak, mahua, *khair*, jackfruit, semal, myrobalan and banyan are some of the trees that grow here. Sal and teak are mainly used to make furniture. Sandalwood is used for making decorative items and fragrant oil.

Thorn and desert forests

Thorn and desert forests thrive in desert conditions with high temperature and low rainfall (between 20 to 80 cm). In India, these forests are found in large parts of Rajasthan, Punjab and Haryana, and some parts of Madhya Pradesh, Maharashtra, Telangana, Andhra Pradesh and Gujarat. The forest cover is scattered and the plants are short with deep roots to help them absorb water from the subsoil. They have spines and glossy leaves to reduce transpiration. Acacia (babul), kikar, date palms, palas and cacti are commonly found here.

Ranthambore forest, Rajasthan

A wetland with mangrove forest

Tidal forests

Tidal forests are also called mangrove forests. They require heavy rainfall of over 200 cm. Tidal forests are found in the deltaic areas. The Ganga-Brahmaputra Delta, the deltas of Mahanadi, the Godavari, the Krishna and the Kaveri are all fringed with mangrove forests. The Sundarbans make up the largest cover of tidal forest. The tidal forests grow in lowlands, which get inundated under sea water during high tides. The trees growing here have stilt-like roots that take in oxygen. These trees are evergreen. The Sundari tree is the dominant species of trees in these forests. Other trees are gorjan, lintal, casuarina, golpata, hogla, hetal and reeds. The mangroves provide an excellent nesting area for many reptiles. The wood obtained from Sundari trees is used to make boats and boxes.

Montane forests

The montane vegetation varies with altitude. It is found in the Himalayan and the Shiwalik regions, that is, in Jammu and Kashmir, Ladakh, Himachal Pradesh, Arunachal Pradesh and Uttarakhand. Tropical deciduous forests are found at the foothills of the Himalayas. Temperate deciduous forests dominate the vegetation on the middle slopes. Coniferous forests are found at a higher altitude.

Montane forest

Sal, oak, ash, beech, chir pine, silver fir, chestnut, cedar, juniper, rhododendrons and deodar are some common species of trees that grow here. They are softwood trees and are used in the paper industry. Alpine vegetation is found 3,500 m above the sea level.

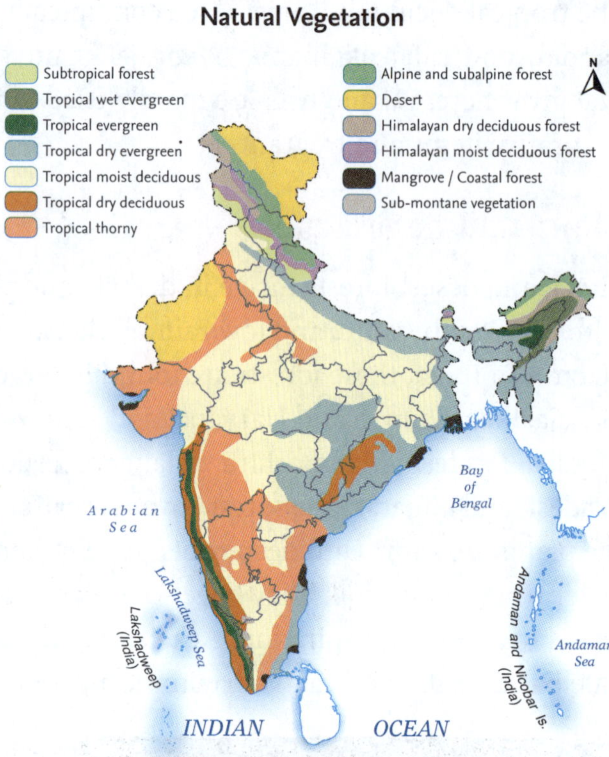

India, Natural Vegetation

Wildlife

A large number of diverse types of animals are found in India.

One-horned rhinoceros

They are usually referred to as fauna. The following chart talks about some important wild animals and the places where they are found.

Animals	Areas where they are found
Royal Bengal tiger	Tidal forest of Sundarbans and monsoon forest of Madhya Pradesh
Elephants	The tropical evergreen forest of Kerala and Assam
One-horned Rhinoceros	Marshy forest areas of Assam and north West Bengal
Asiatic Lion	Dry deciduous forests of Gir
Indian Bison	Tropical deciduous forests of Peninsular India

Conservation of Forest Cover

Forests are extremely valuable to us. They play a major role as they have both environmental as well as economic value. The government of India has developed a law to protect and preserve the natural habitat of the wild animals. National parks, wildlife sanctuaries and bioreserves are developed to protect our natural vegetation and wildlife. There are 14 bioreserves, 450 wildlife sanctuaries and 89 national parks in India.

The different awareness programs taken up to encourage community participation to conserve flora and fauna are:

i. Social forestry

ii. *Vanmahotsav*

The Indian government has passed laws against the trade as well as killing of birds and animals. In India, killing of lions, tiger, deer, great Indian bustards, one-horned rhinoceroses and peacocks is illegal. These animals are poached for collection and illegal trade of hides, skins, nails, feathers and so on. Thus, it becomes essential to protect these animals by law.

The term social forestry was introduced by J.C.Westoby. It aimed to benefit both the rural and urban areas. It is primarily a government-based programme with the objective of helping in environment, social and rural development. The National Commission on Agriculture has classified social forestry into three categories—urban forestry, rural forestry and farm forestry. Social forestry aims to increase forest cover by common people to meet the growing demand of timber, fuel wood and fodder to reduce pressure on the traditional forest area.

Geo Connect

China is a vast country and has a diverse climate. It experiences different temperatures and varying amounts of rainfall in different parts. It experiences continental monsoon. In June, south China receives rainfall which is known as 'plum rain'. The winters are cold and dry whereas the summers are hot and rainy.

In a Nutshell

- India has a tropical monsoon climate.
- The factors affecting the climate of India are latitude, height above the sea level, the Northern Mountains and the distance from the sea.
- India has four main seasons—the cold dry season, the hot dry season, the hot wet season and the retreating monsoon season.
- India receives most of its rainfall from the southwest monsoon.

Workout

A. Fill in the blanks with the correct answers.

1. The coastal regions experience .... climate.

   a. cold　b. hot　c. dry　d. equable

2. .... is the coldest month of the year in India.

   a. March　b. January　c. February　d. April

3. .... is the local wind experienced in Assam and Bengal.
   a. Kalbaisakhi b. Loo c. Mango showers d. Monsoon wind
4. Monsoon in India does not occur in the month of ....
   a. October b. November c. September d. March
5. The southwest monsoon has .... branches.
   a. two b. three c. six d. five

B. Complete this table.

Forest	Climate	Distribution	Important trees
Tropical monsoon forest			
			Mahogany, rosewood
Mountain			
	Need heavy rainfall of about 200 cm		
		Rajasthan	

C. Answer these questions in brief.

1. What are jet streams?
2. Write a short note on the branches of the southwest monsoon.
3. What are western disturbances?
4. What kind of climate does India have?

D. Answer these questions in detail.

1. Explain the factors that affect the climate of a place.
2. Explain the approach and the retreating of the monsoon winds in India.
3. What are main features of the tropical evergreen and deciduous forests?
4. Write a short note on the wildlife of India.
5. Why is it important to conserve forests?

Think Box

Name two states of India that receive rainfall during winters. What is the cause of winter rainfall in these states?

Picture Study

Look at the picture and answer the questions.

1. This is a picture of Royal Bengal Tigers. Where in India are these animals found?
2. Name two more animals that are endemic to India.

Life Skills and Values

All living things are interdependent. Therefore, they should live in harmony with each other. With the help of your language teacher and geography teacher, create a 'Thank You Card' for all the people in the community without whom your environment would not have been clean.

Enjoy

Select six states, including the state you stay in, and find out the similarities in flora, fauna and the climate. Using a transparent sheet, superimpose the three maps and explain the relation between the flora, fauna and climate in a short report and present it in class.

Weblinks

For more information, visit
https://www.newworldencyclopedia.org/entry/Climate_of_India
Last accessed on 31/July/2020

15 India: Human Resources

Let's learn about...

- human resources and human capital.
- distribution of population in India.
- role of health and education in developing human resources.
- skilled and unskilled human resources.

Key Terms

- human resources
- human capital
- education
- population distribution
- population pyramid

Reflect

Read the passage and answer the question.

Lakshita is a semi-skilled worker in a cement factory. She is very efficient. Her husband is a household worker. They have two kids and live in the worker's colony where living conditions are not good. Recognizing Lakshita's capabilities, the company plans to train her to increase her potential and improve her living conditions. Her organization has certain schemes to impart education to those workers who are efficient but lack proper skills.

Q. Why do you think the company plans to train Lakshita?

Human Resources

Human resources comprise people who form the bulk of the productive population, commonly referred to as the workforce of a country. Human resources are also known as human capital. Human capital refers to the induced productive quality of the labour force. Human resources can be made more productive through better education, skill development and health facilities. We have understood from the example of Lakshita that skill is an important parameter for assessing the quality of human resources. People can be turned into valuable assets through investments in,

Educated human resources are an asset to the country

- Education
- Healthcare

When the existing human resource is further developed by giving higher education and healthcare, it is called human capital formation.

The Ministry of Human Resources and Development looks after the welfare of human resources of India. Every organization and corporate firm also has a dedicated department for human resource development. It looks after the welfare of the people working in that organization.

Human capital formation

Human capital formation deals with the acquired capabilities of individuals that are developed through formal and informal education at home and school, and through in-service training and work experience. The Government of India invests in human capital formation by improving healthcare and education to improve the capabilities of its human resources. This helps the country to increase its productive workforce, which in turn results in its socio-economic development. The Government of India has initiated many educational and social welfare schemes to enable people to raise their standard of living considerably.

FactPedia

Jacob Mincer is known as the father of labour economics. He thought of human capital as the stock of knowledge, habits, social and personality attributes, including creativity embodied in the ability to perform labour in order to produce economic value.

Quality of Human Resources

Every individual is considered as a potential human resource. The quality of human resource depends upon literacy rate, national health and skill acquired by the people of that country. An educated and healthy population is an asset to the country.

Education

Have you ever wondered why our parents send us to school? This is because education opens new horizons for us. It contributes to the growth of an individual, who in turn contributes towards the growth of the country. India has various schemes to provide both elementary and higher education. The Sarva Shiksha Abhiyan is a remarkable step taken by the Government of India to provide elementary education to all children in the age group of six to fifteen. The University Grants Commission (UGC) takes care of higher education through distance learning programmes and by opening universities. The government also has various schemes to impart vocational education to develop specific work-related skills.

Literacy

Literacy is the foundation and key component of socio-economic progress of any country. According to the census, a person is considered literate if he or she can read or write and understand any one language. There has been a steady improvement of the literacy rate in India from the 1911 census to the 2011 census. It shows a steady growth from 52.21 per cent to 74.04 per cent.

DIY

Study the table and answer the questions.

#	State	Literacy	Male	Female	% Change
-	India	74.04	82.14	65.46	8.66
1	Kerala	94.00	96.11	92.07	3.14
2	Lakshadweep	81.85	95.56	87.95	5.19
3	Mizoram	91.33	93.35	89.27	2.53
4	Goa	88.70	92.65	84.66	6.69
5	Tripura	87.22	91.53	82.73	14.03
6	Daman and Diu	87.10	91.54	79.55	8.92
7	Andaman and Nicobar Islands	86.63	90.27	82.43	5.66
8	Delhi	86.21	90.94	80.76	4.54
9	Chandigarh	86.05	89.99	81.19	4.11

1. What is literacy rate?
2. Which state has the highest literacy rate in India?
3. What do you think can be done to increase the literacy rates in states?

Health

Health is an asset to an individual and a healthy person is an asset to the country. Our government has implemented different policies to improve the accessibility of healthcare and family welfare with a special focus on the deprived segment of the society. India has built up a huge health infrastructure over the years. Many Indian villages are well-equipped with primary health units and community health centres.

Skilled and unskilled labour

Skilled labour refers to the workforce, which requires a specialized skill to complete a specialized task. Skilled labour involves advanced knowledge, training and a specialized skill set. Electricians plumbers, teachers, lawyers, doctors, and engineers belong to this category. **Unskilled labour** refers to the workforce that has limited skill. They do physical work that does not depend on technical ability or skills. Usually, they work as daily wage workers at construction sites and industries or as rickshaw pullers.

Distribution of Population in India

Density of population is the number of people living in a unit area. It is expressed in person per square kilometre. India has 382 persons per square kilometre. The way in which people are spread across the country is known as the pattern of distribution of population. The distribution of population depends on physical and economic factors. Geographical or physical factors include the quality of land, availability of water and climatic conditions. Economic factors include industrial development, infrastructural facilities and connectivity of the place. We have already learnt in the previous chapter that India is a geographically diverse country. Study the following table to understand the density of population and the factors influencing the distribution of population.

Density of Population	Geographical Reasons	States
Densely populated 300 persons per sq km	Fertile soil suitable for agriculture with abundant rainfall and sufficient irrigation facility	Punjab, Uttar Pradesh, Bihar, West Bengal, Kerala, Tamil Nadu
Medium density populated 100 to 300 persons per sq km	Industrial areas and the region around the main ports	Gujarat, Maharashtra, Goa, Karnataka, Odisha and Tamil Nadu
Sparsely populated less than 100 persons per sq km	The areas with low rainfall and hilly undulating terrain region	Thar Desert and hilly regions of the north and northeast

The population growth and distribution of population in India are influenced by various factors as shown in the flow chart.

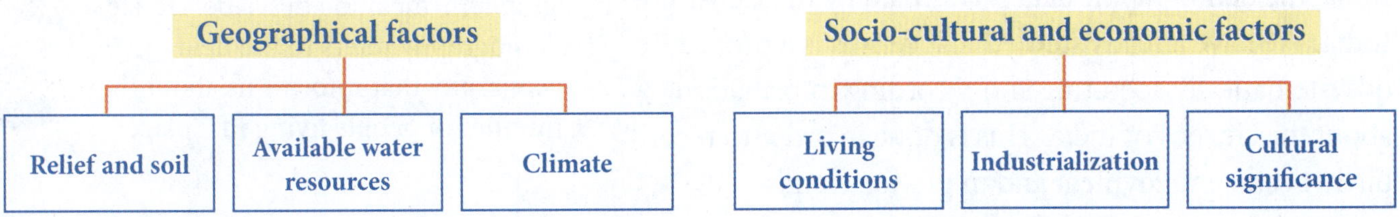

Population Study

The study of population is very important for the country's development. Population is analyzed based on characteristics such as urbanization, rural and urban population, migration, government polices and demography.

Urbanization: India has experienced significant urbanization in the recent years due to rapid industrialization and globalization. Rural lifestyles are giving way to more comfortable lives in cities, with better job opportunities and improved standards of living. Rapid urbanization is significantly transforming the Indian society. Urban areas have better infrastructure, medical facilities and social amenities. People feel they can lead better lives in cities and thus, they migrate.

Rural and urban population: People living in the urban centres constitute the urban population, whereas people living in the rural sector make up the rural population. India is basically an agricultural country, which is why most of the population of India, nearly 72 per cent, is concentrated in the villages.

Migration: Migration is one of the most notable and visible characteristics of human population in India as well as in the entire world. Migration has influenced the human population distribution and its character. You will find that many rickshaw pullers, vegetable vendors and daily wage labourers are from nearby village areas. The lack of job opportunities and poor infrastructural facilities in rural areas is slowly pushing the rural population to the urban areas. If you visit an unplanned urban area, which is referred to as a slum, you will find a huge number of people from the rural areas, who had moved to the city with the expectation of better living conditions. This has changed the pattern of urban population in a huge way. Migration also takes place from city to city and from town to town. Natural calamities also force the people to migrate from the affected area to a safer region. For example, a considerable amount of population migrated from Bhuj to Ahmedabad after the 2001 Gujarat earthquake.

Figure Out

Name four major urban settlements in India.

Government development policies: The government undertakes new projects, such as, building dams, setting up industries, building roads and railway tracks. These projects influence the demographic pattern of the country. They also need a huge labour force. This leads to the development of small townships to provide housing facilities to the people who will work there. Many cities have been established near major industrial centres.

Pattern of population: Demography is the systematic study of population. Demographic data helps the government to form policies related to health management, education, public welfare and economic development. In India, the demographic data is collected by the Census of India. We have already studied that census is a procedure of systematically acquiring and recording information about the citizens of India. This is done in order to record birth, death, employment and migration trends.

FactPedia

The word 'demography' is of Greek origin and is composed of two words, 'demos' meaning people and 'graphein' meaning describe. Hence, demography refers to the field of geography that informs us about the number of people living in a place.

Population Pyramid

We have already studied about the two important characteristics of population composition, that is, age and sex, along with literacy level, health conditions and income level. The population composition refers to the structure of the population. An interesting way of studying the population composition of a country is to analyze the population pyramid, which is based on age and sex ratio. Let us understand this with the help of these examples.

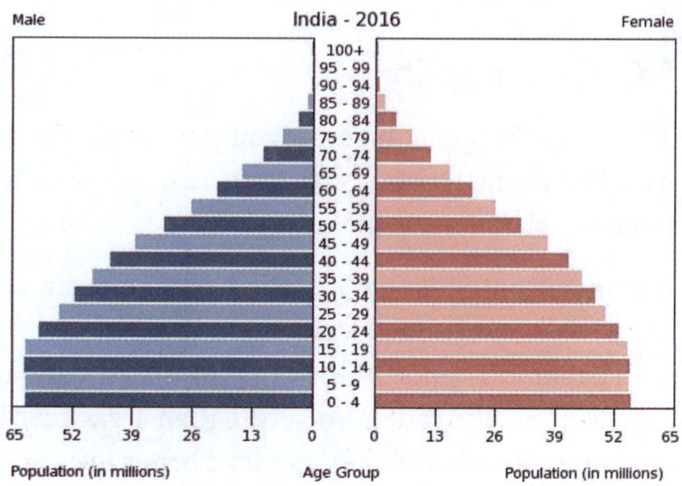

Population pyramid of India

Population Pyramid of the United States of America

The population pyramid of USA has a narrow base, which denotes low birth rates. Decrease in death rate denotes that more people exist in the old age category. Industrialization, urbanization and a rising standard of living lead to a decline in the birth rate. Therefore, the concentration of the people in the middle and the older age groups is more. Developed countries such as Japan have a similar population pyramid.

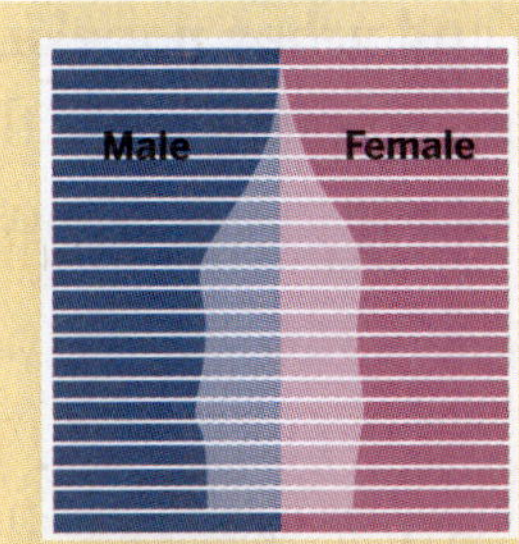

Population pyramid of the United States

Population Pyramid of Ghana

The population pyramid of Ghana is broad at the base and it rapidly narrows down towards the top. This denotes that many children are born but a large number of them die soon after their birth. Thus, relatively few attain adult age and even fewer people attain their old age. You will find similar pyramids in underdeveloped countries like Kenya.

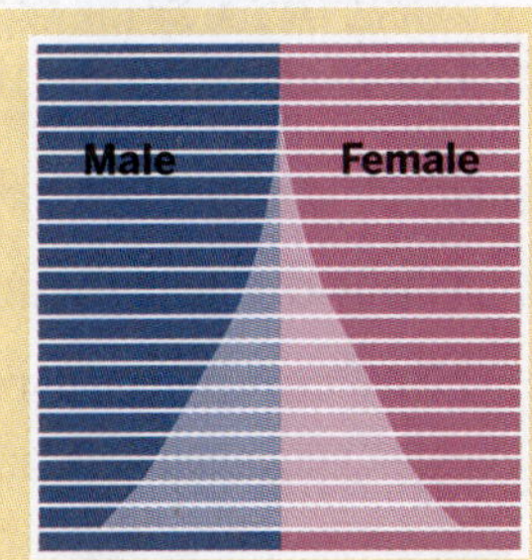

Population pyramid of Ghana

Geo Connect

The United Nations Development Programme (UNDP) supports development strategies to combat poverty by proper resource management to enhance economic opportunities. UNDP sponsors various projects related to development, such as effective water supply and sanitation, women's education and emancipation.

In a Nutshell

- Human resources is the driving force of a country's development.
- Educated, skilled and healthy human resources are the future assets of a country.
- Human resources help transform natural resources into useful products.
- Greater number of skilled people leads to better and efficient utilization of resources.

Workout

A. Fill in the blanks with the correct answers.

1. Human resource is also referred to as ....
   a. workforce b. labour force c. human capital d. All of the above
2. .... is densely populated.
   a. Gujarat b. Goa c. Kerala d. Odisha

3. The word 'demography' is of .... origin.
   a. English b. Greek c. German d. None of the above
4. 72 per cent of India's population is concentrated in ....
   a. cities b. towns c. villages d. All of the above

B. Write T for true and F for false.

1. Relief of a place determines its population density. ☐
2. Rural areas have better infrastructure. ☐
3. Demography is the systematic study of population. ☐
4. Population pyramid of the USA has a broad base. ☐

C. Answer these questions in brief.

1. What do you mean by 'human resource'?
2. How can human resource be made more productive?
3. On what does the quality of human resource depend?
4. Define:
   a. Literate person b. Census c. Density of population

D. Answer these questions in detail.

1. Explain human capital formation.
2. How does education contribute towards the growth of a nation?
3. Write a short note on population pyramid.
4. Differentiate between:
   a. Skilled and unskilled labour
   b. Population pyramid of a developed country and population pyramid of an underdeveloped country
   c. Rural population and urban population

Think Box

Find out about the different schemes of the government related to skill development and employment.

Picture Study

Look at the picture and answer the questions.

1. Which of these factors is most important for the human resources of a country?
2. How can a country train its human resources.

Life Skills and Values

A. Indian agriculture changed drastically after the Green Revolution. Green Revolution stands as an exemplary instance of how human capital can contribute towards the country's development. Similarly, the advancement in the IT sector also stands as a testimony of the value of human capital. Arrange a panel discussion on the contribution of human capital towards the country's development. Invite teachers and students to join the conversation.

B. Pay a visit to the nearby Primary Health Centre (PHC) and find out the following details.

1. Who is in charge of the PHC?
2. How many doctors and nurses work there?
3. How are they linked with the main hospital in the nearby city or town?

Enjoy

Conduct a survey at you school and collect the following data for the last three years:

1. Number of admissions
2. Number of girls enrolled
3. Number of boys enrolled

Using the data collected, draw a bar graph and explain the change of trend over a time of three years.

Weblinks

For more information, visit
http://mhrd.gov.in/#main-content
Last accessed on 31/July/2020

Across the Boundary 4

A. India is an amazing land with a rich cultural heritage and amazing geographical features. Most of us would have heard the term 'Incredible India'. Develop a catalogue on Incredible India. You can include the following features.

- Geographical diversity.
- Historical heritage
- Modern-day scientific achievements along with ancient knowledge and wisdom
- New developments for maintaining a balance between environmental protection and development
- Sustainable development in India.

Take the help of your geography teacher, history teacher, and science teacher to make this catalogue. Give a suitable title to your catalogue.

B. Have you ever seen the polio vaccine awareness programme? Why do you think the Government of India spends on the documentaries related to health, vaccination, road safety and so on?

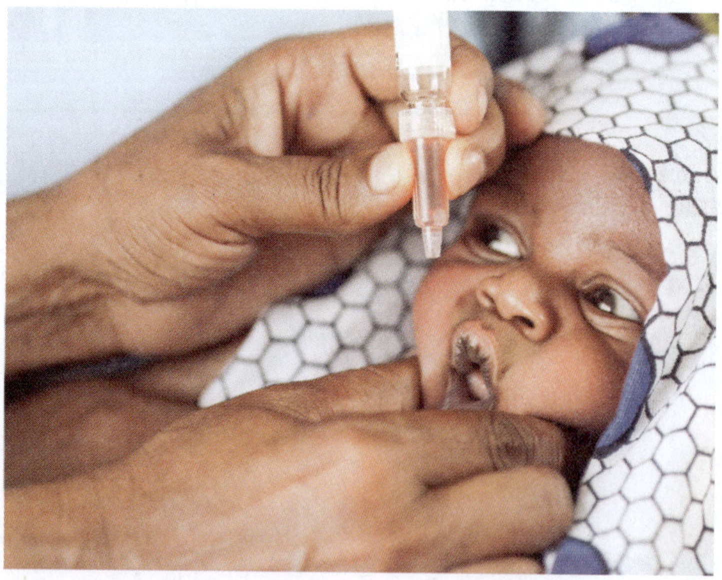

Snap Recap

The Snap Recap section contains a collection of mind maps that draw the outline of the concepts that you have learned in this book. Mind mapping is a useful technique that helps you learn more effectively and improves the way that you record information. They help you see the way pieces of information fit together. Mind maps also help you remember information, as they hold it in a format that your mind finds easy to recall.

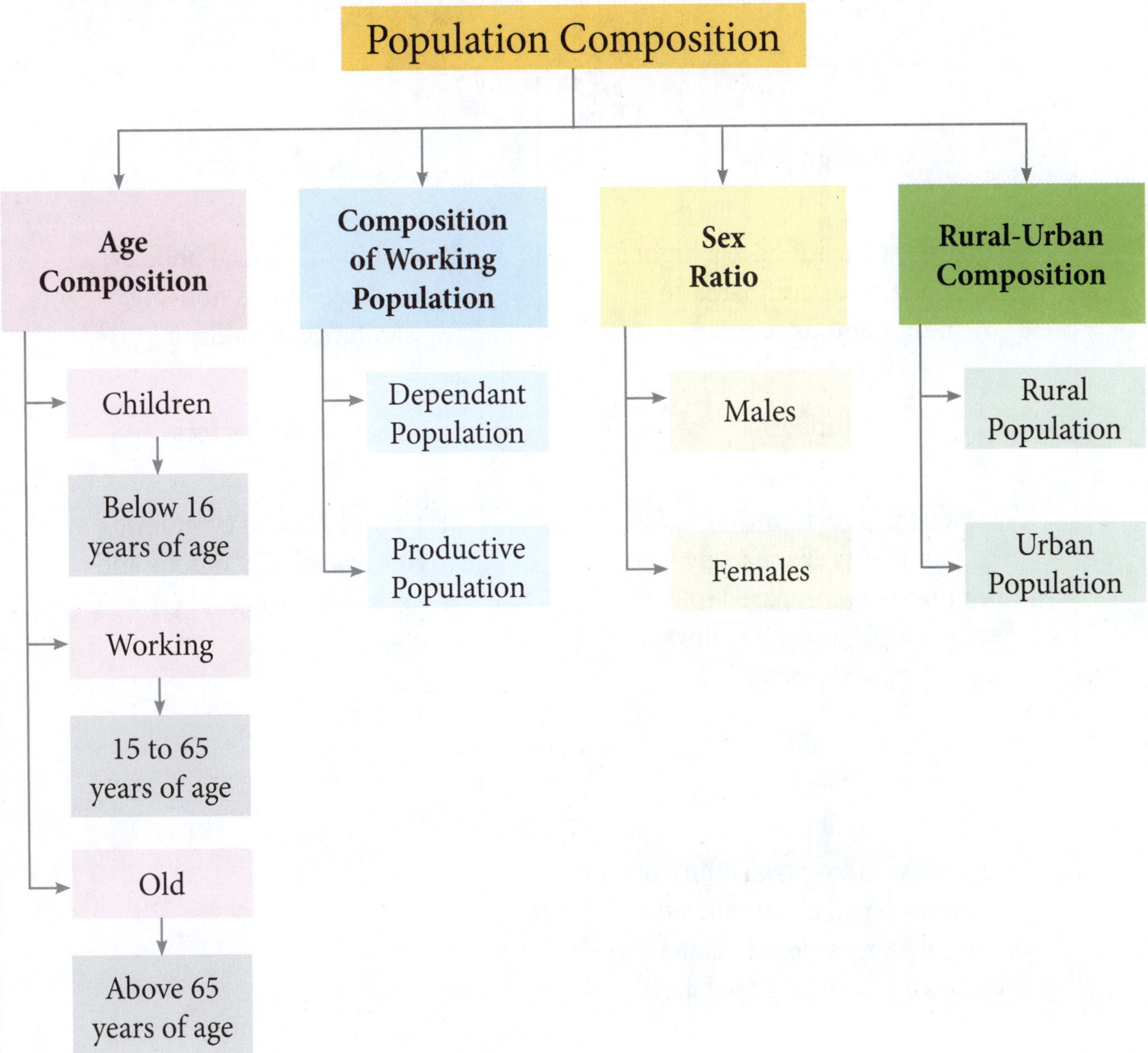

Factors Affecting Distribution of Population

- **Geographical Factors**
  - Topography
    - Plains and plateaus have a higher population as compared to mountainous regions.
  - Climate
    - Regions with extreme climatic conditions are sparsely populated as compared to the regions with moderate climatic conditions.
  - Water
    - Regions with low availability of water are sparsely populated, whereas areas close to water bodies are densely populated.
  - Soil and Minerals
    - Fertility of the soil also affects the distribution of population
- **Socio-economic Factors**
  - Social Factors
    - Ease of living, social policies, affordable living, housing, sanitation, healthcare
  - Economic Factors
    - Type and scale of economic activity, availability of jobs and high wages

Causes of Urbanization

Geographical Factors	caused by high birth rate or migration; main cause of urbanization
Industrialization	new commercial enterprises create new jobs in cities, mostly in developing nations
Rural-Urban Transformation	higher per capita income creates need for better housing; developers make new houses; rapid development of housing and urban infrastructure
Employment Opportunities	urban centres provide better employment opportunities; rural to urban migration; unplanned urban growth
Education	rural to urban migration for seeking better educational facilities; towns and big cities have better educations institutions
Standard of Living	living and property costs are higher in the main city; encourages countryside development
Transportation	transportation routes open access to urban centres; construction of expressways and highways; rapid outgrowth, urban sprawl

Disaster Management

- **Hazard**: dangerous condition or event; has the potential of causing injury to life; may be natural or manmade
- **Capacity**: resources, means and strength that enable communities and households to cope, withstand, mitigate or quickly recover from a disaster
- **Vulnerability**: the extent to which a geographic area, structure, community and services are likely to be damaged or disrupted by the impact of a particular hazard
- **Risk**: the measure of expected losses due to a hazard occurring in a particular area at a specific time.

TEST YOURSELF I

Full Marks: 50

A. Fill in the blanks. 1×10=10

1. .... is a smart city.
2. Deepwater Horizon oil spill occurred on .... in the ...., near ....
3. The natural events caused due to overflow of water is called ....
4. ASDMA stands for ....
5. .... faults caused the Nepal Earthquake of 2015.
6. The strait that separates Asia from North America is the ....
7. The systematic study of population is called ....
8. .... in Asia has a Mediterranean-type of climate.
9. The longitudinal valley located in the Shiwalik Range is the ....
10. The gradual withdrawal of the monsoon wind is called ....

B. Fill in the blanks with the correct answers. 1×5=5

1 Jamshedpur is a ....

a. urban suburb
b. manufacturing town
c. entertainment town
d. defence town

2. An earthquake is a .... disaster.

a. meteorological
b. geophysical
c. climatological
d. man-made

3. Brahmaputra has .... tributaries.

a. 20
b. 41
c. 12
d. 0

4. The epicenter of the Nepal earthquake was located in ....

a. Kathmandu
b. Lamjung
c. Pokhara
d. Butwal

5. Rhodoliths are ....

a. fish
b. stones
c. seaweed assemblages
d. corals

C. Give reasons for the following: 2×6=12

1. London is one of the most expensive cities in the world.
2. The community should be trained to reduce the impact of disasters.

3. Mitigation is an important activity before disasters.
4. State, district and local bodies play an important role in disaster management
5. The gulf oil spill is documented as one of the worst disasters in US history.
6. Southwest monsoon played a major role in the Assam floods.

D. Differentiate between these terms. 2×4=8

1. Educational centers and entertainment centers
2. Risk and vulnerability
3. Cabinet Committee on Security and National Institute of Disaster Management
4. Bioremediation and ISB

E. Answer in one word. 1×5=5

1. Cities that grow due to their rich history.
2. Epicenter of Nepal Earthquake.
3. Two international organizations involved in disaster management.
4. Release of petroleum products in marine environment.
5. A constant vigilant watch carried out by village youth after a disaster.

F. Write short notes on the following. 1×5=5

1. Manchurian type of climate
2. The Karakoram Range
3. Temperate Grassland
4. The taiga
5. The Islands of India

G. Look at the picture and answer the questions. (*Any one*) 5

a.

1. Identify the structure shown in the picture. Where is it found the most? 2
2. What is the function of such a structure? 1
3. This place was hit by a major disaster recently. What was the main cause of the disaster? 2

b. 

1. Identify the animal and state where you can find it. 1
2. State the climatic characteristics of this region. 2
3. Explain in brief the natural vegetation of this region. 2

TEST YOURSELF II

Full Marks: 50

A. Look at the map and answer the questions. 5

1. Identify the area shown.
2. This region was affected by an earthquake in 2015. What were the main causes of that earthquake?
3. What were the effects of this disaster?

B. Answer these questions in brief. 1×5=5

1. What is disaster management?
2. What is the aim of disaster management?
3. Name two disasters that have hit south-east Asia.
4. Why is the Deepwater Horizon oil spill named so? Where did it happen?
5. What are the various methods of removing oil from the marine environment?

C. Fill in the blanks. 1×5=5

1. Asia makes up the eastern part of .... supercontinent.
2. .... and .... separates India from Sri Lanka.
3. The key component of a country's socioeconomic progress is ....

4. .... is the local wind experienced in Karnataka.

5. Natural calamities force people to.............................. to different areas.

D. Fill in the blanks with correct answers. 1×5=5

1. .... plateau is surrounded by Tien Shan on the west and Altai on the north.

a. Mekong
b. Mongolian
c. Deccan
d. None of the above

2. The animals of the tundra region have thick fur to ....

a. make them attractive
b. keep them warm
c. to protect them from lichen
d. all of the above

3. The difference between the day and night temperatures in the tropical desert region is ....

a. high
b. low
c. same
d. negligible

4. .... originate in the Mediterranean region and visit India during the winter.

a. Western disturbances
b. Jet stream
c. Loo
d. Mango showers

5. The major productive population of the country is referred as ....

a. human resources
b. population
c. educated people
d. all of the above.

E. Give reasons for the following: 2×5=10

1. Natural vegetation is sparse in the tundra region.
2. The equatorial region has low range of climate.
3. The rivers of Deccan region are unsuitable for irrigation
4. The Himalayas plays an important role for modifying the climate of India.

F. Differentiate between: 2×5=10

1. Taiga type of climate and equatorial type of climate.
2. Skilled labour and unskilled labour
3. Malwa Plateau and Deccan plateau
4. Lesser Himalaya and Greater Himalaya
5. Eastern Coastal plains and Western Coastal Plain

G. Name the following: 1×5=5

1. The strait that separates Asia from North America
2. The systematic study of population.
3. A region in Asia which has Mediterranean type of climate.

4. The longitudinal valley located in the Shiwalik Range.
5. The gradual withdrawal of the monsoon wind.

H. Map Work 5

On the map of Asia, mark the following:

a. The Roof of the world
b. The Northern Lowlands
c. The capital of Bangladesh
d. Hindukush Mountain
e. The strait that separates Asia from North America.

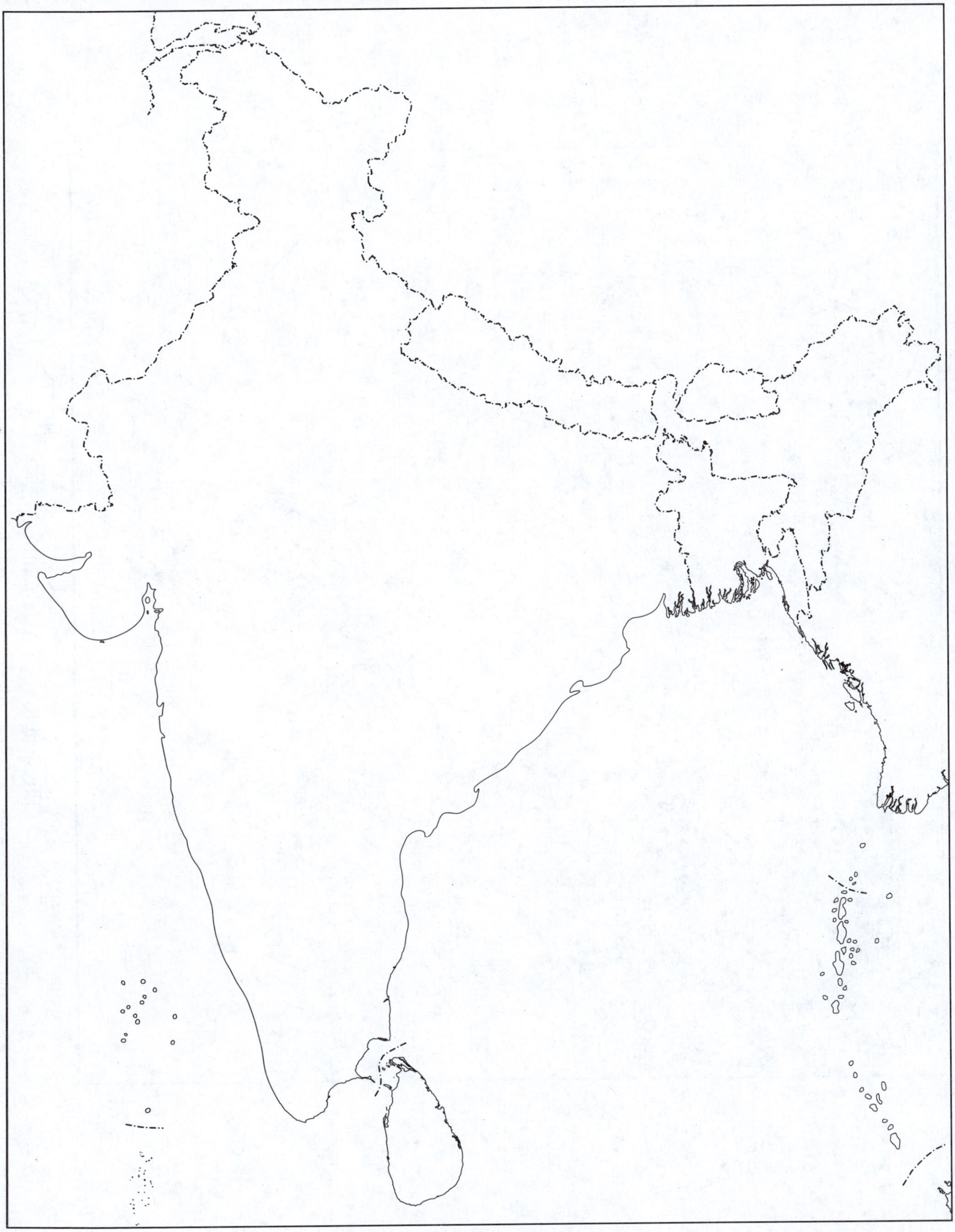

Physical Map of India-Outline

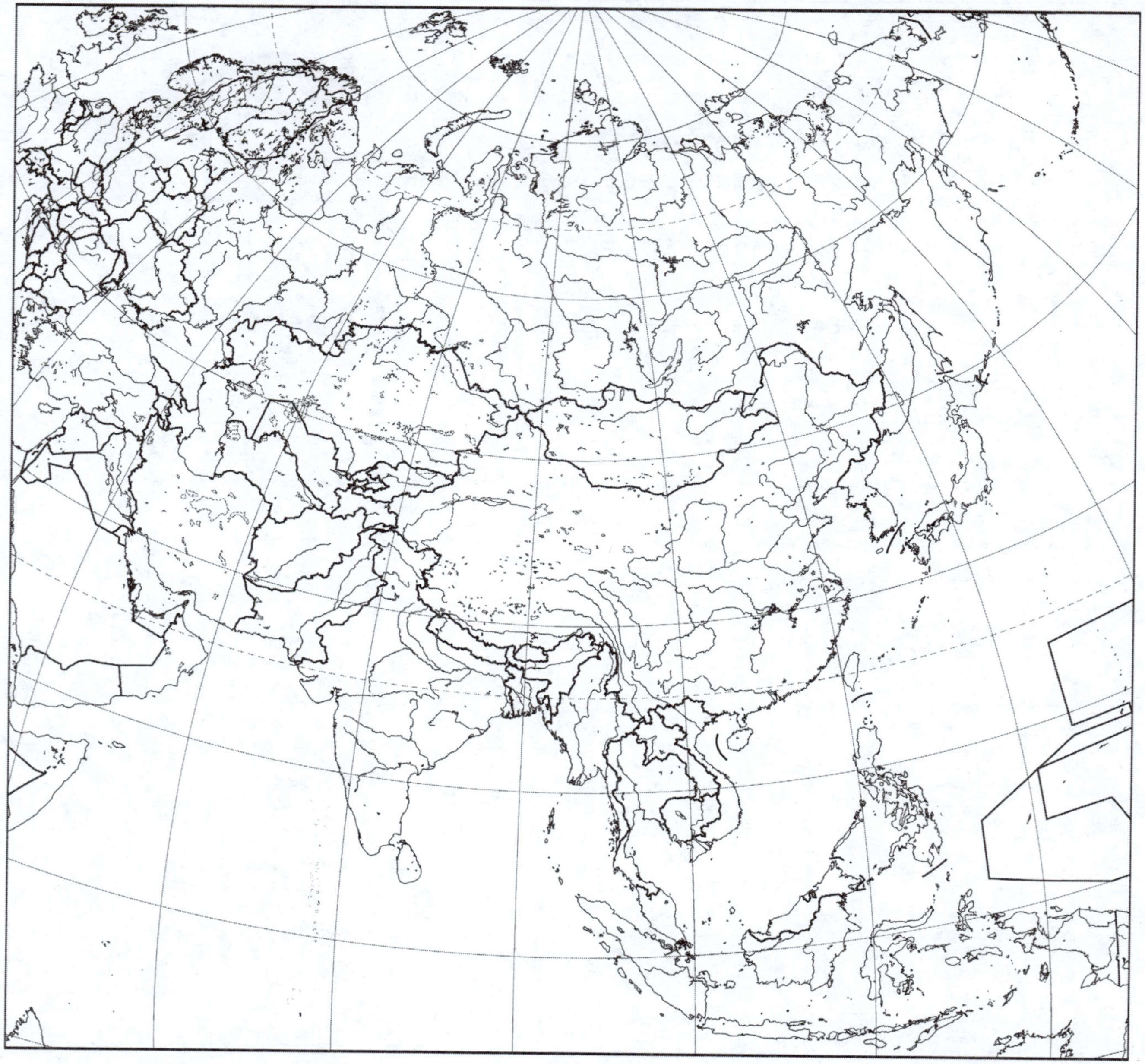

Physical Map of Asia-Outline